TOWARD SPIRITUAL SOVEREIGNTY

A Secular Bible

by

John W. Casperson

authorHOUSE®

AuthorHouse™
1663 Liberty Drive, Suite 200
Bloomington, IN 47403
www.authorhouse.com
Phone: 1-800-839-8640

First published by AuthorHouse   7/27/2007

ISBN: 978-1-4343-1571-7 (sc)
ISBN: 978-1-4343-1570-0 (hc)

Library of Congress Control Number: 2007903575

Printed in the United States of America
Bloomington, Indiana

This book is printed on acid-free paper.

CONTENTS

PROLOGUE

"Make your own bible. Select and collect all the words and sentences that in all your readings have been to you like the blast of a trumpet."
– American Essayist and poet, Ralph Waldo Emerson (1803-1882).

Forces of the 14th -16th century European Renaissance brought revolutionary change to people of the continent which has influenced western art, culture, and society ever since. The Renaissance (rebirth) gave unparalleled expression to the artistic genius of the era and formed a foundation for the Age of Enlightenment (18th century) that followed. Forces of the 16th century protestant Reformation brought revolutionary change to western Christian religious theology that changed the landscape of Divine worship. It is now time for a New Reformation to be accompanied by a New Renaissance of creativity in art, and more significantly, a New Renaissance pertaining to how we can begin to worship Divinity and *each other* and honor the life force of flora and fauna with whom we share this planet.

Every human being (Homo Divinitas, person of spirit) is of divine inspiration. If realized through a religious creed, the act of worshipping our Creator would limit formal worship to the defined number of established religions in the same way astrology divides

1

people among twelve astrological signs. One can assume that God/ Allah/ the Great Integrity did not intend for Homo Divinitas to play a celestial form of follow the leader the way rodents followed the Pied Piper of Hamelin. Billions of persons who have existed, now exist, and shall exist, must have unlimited access to all schools of thought, philosophy, and theology in order to be a self-ordained individual "church". Thomas Paine (1737-1809) who authored *Common Sense* and *The Rights of Man* said, "My mind is my own church." Spiritual growth, worship and emulation of God/Allah/the Great Integrity may then occur freely without religious fetter and judgment. Spiritual fulfillment may be sought within the realm of one's own native spirituality. Spiritual fulfillment can be achieved with moral and ethical behavior that is within the capacity of all human beings.

PART ONE
HOMO DIVINITAS

CHAPTER 1
THE FIVE CONCEPTS OF HOMO DIVINITAS

"The greatest tragedy in mankind's entire history may be the hijacking of morality by religion."
– Arthur C. Clarke.

This author first put forth five concepts of native spirituality in *A New Reformation.* These spiritual Truths should be considered self-evident and inalienable, not subject to compromise, infringement, or monopoly by established religious doctrine or established governmental legislation. Homo Divinitas has the right to establish his or her own spiritual base, spiritual direction, and spiritual reach, i.e. his or her own "religion".

Prior to enumerating the five concepts, "truth" should be fully understood and appreciated thus must be qualified and quantified. Parmenides of ancient Greece, circa 510 B.C. – 450 B.C., was one of the most significant pre-Socratic philosophers. The seed of Idealist philosophy germinated in the ancient Greek colony of Elea in the Village of Lucania on the western coast of Italy in the 5th century before Christ. Though Xenophanes founded the Eleatic school of thought, Parmenides is considered a prime exemplar of that school. Parmenides endeavored to use metaphysics as a means to interpret, quantify, and understand the mystery of, and distinctions between, noumenon (an object perceived by intellect or reason alone), and phenomenon (an observable event or object). Indeed, Plato himself in the *Sophist* refers to the work of "our father Parmenides" as something to be respected. Parmenides has influenced the history of Western Philosophy and is often seen as its grandfather. "Possibly as a recreational aside in a busy life he composed a philosophical poem *On Nature* of which 160 verses survive, enough to regret that Parmenides did not write prose. The poet announces with a twinkle in his eye, that a goddess has delivered to him a revelation: that all things are one; that motion, change, and development are unreal – phantasms of superficial, contradictory, untrustworthy sense; that beneath these mere appearances lies an unchanging, homogeneous, indivisible, indissoluble, motionless unity, which is the only Being, the only Truth, and the only God."[1] That Parmenides directly and inseparably equates Truth with God is significant. Significant too, is his awareness of the phantasmic nature of untrustworthy sense, with which we perceive each other, our ethos, and our God.

That something is true extends beyond semantic or etymological terms such as factual, accurate, correct, or valid. Pragmata (affairs, occurrences) can be true when in alignment with purpose such as being true of heart (love) or true of mind (fidelity). Such is the case when word resonates with authenticity of deed and deed resonates with authenticity of word, each under the aegis of conscience. Philosophically, at least nine theories attempt to explain truth, what truth is, and what is meant by truth. Great minds, from Socrates, Plato, and Aristotle, to Spinoza, Hegel, and Dewey, have attempted to define truth, each pertinent, each in their own way. One of the ringleaders when "rounding up the usual suspects" in the crime of hijacking morality by religion (to which Arthur C. Clarke refers) would be Saint Augustine of Hippo (354-430). Though living 800 years after Parmenides, Augustine was at least as eloquent as Parmenides, if not more so, when he attempted to define truth. This author is confounded and concerned with most views espoused by Augustine much in the same manner Sherlock Holmes was vexed by his nemesis, Professor Moriarty. Provocative and ironic it is, that this author has excoriated and vilified Augustine in this and previous work, yet his definition of truth is profoundly accurate and encompassing. Credit is given when credit is due thus the thoughts of Augustine follow:

1. Truth exists: - It is self-defeating to deny the existence of truth. If someone claims that "Truth does not exist", then we can counter by asking if the claim is True or False. If the claim is false, then Truth exists, and if the claim is True, then Truth exists.

2. Truth is unchangeable: - It is impossible for truth to change. What is true today always has been and always will be true. All true propositions are immutable truths. Pragmatic views of truth that imply that what is true today may be false tomorrow are untrue. If truth changes, than pragmatism will be untrue tomorrow, if indeed it could ever be true.

3. Truth is eternal: - By extension of its Unchangeable nature, Truth must be Eternal. Even if every created thing ceases to exist, Truth will continue to exist. But suppose someone asks. "What if truth itself should someday perish?" Then the truth that "Truth has perished" would still exist eternally. Any denial of the eternity of truth turns out to be an affirmation of its eternity.

4. Truth is spiritual: - The existence of truth presupposes the existence of minds. Without a mind, truth could not exist. The object of knowledge is a meaningful thought, which resides in one or more minds.

   a) Truth is not a function of matter; - The existence of truth is incompatible with any materialistic view of man. Materialists believe that all thinking and reasoning is merely the result of the motion of particles in the brain. But one set of relative physical motions is not truer than another set. Therefore, if there is no mind, there can be no truth; and if there is no truth, materialism cannot be true. Truth cannot be a function of the position of material objects because if a thought was a result of some physical motion in the brain, no two persons could have the same thought. A physical motion is a fleeting event different from every other motion. Two persons could not have the same random motion, nor could one person have the same random motion twice.

   b) Truth is not a function of time: - If thoughts were the result of physical motions in the brain, memory and communication would be impossible. We are able to recall the past because we have minds and not because of the motion of particles in our brains. Thus, if one is able to think the same thought twice, truth must be independent of time.

   c) Truth is not a function of space: - Truth is independent of Space as well. Not only does truth defy time and matter; it defies space as well. For communication to be possible between two or more people, the identical truth must be in two or more minds at the same time. If, in opposition, anyone wished to deny that an immaterial idea could exist in two different minds at the same time, his denial must be conceived to exist in his own mind only; and since it has not registered in any other mind, it does not occur to us to refute it!

5) Truth is Superior to the human mind: - By its very nature, truth cannot be subjective and individualistic. Truth is immutable, but the human mind is changeable. Even though beliefs vary from one person to another, truth itself cannot change. Moreover, the human mind does not stand in judgment of truth; rather truth judges our reason. While we sometimes judge other human minds (as we say for example, that someone's mind is not as keen as it should be), we do not judge truth. If truth and the human mind were equal, truth could not be eternal and immutable since the human mind is finite, mutable and subject to error. Therefore, truth must transcend human reason; truth must be superior to any individual human mind as well as to the sum total of human minds. From this it follows that there must be a mind higher than the human mind in which truth resides.

6) Truth is God: - We have seen that Truth exists, is unchangeable, eternal, spiritual, and is superior to the human mind. But only God possesses these attributes. If we substitute the word "God" for the word "Truth" in the list of attributes, we see that: God Exists, God is Unchangeable, God is eternal, God is Spiritual, God is not a function of Space, Time, or Matter, God is superior to the human mind.

These attributes apply equally to Truth and God, and only to Truth and God. Truth and God are identical. Truth and God are convertible. Truth is God. God is truth. No created thing possesses the attributes of Truth or God. There can be no True propositions about created entities, including numbers, geometric patterns, or so-called "laws" of science because they are all dependent on Space, Time, or Matter. The only true propositions are about God. In other words, Knowing Truth is knowing God. Truth is Knowledge of God."[2]

Spiritually, Homo Divinitas, by virtue of his Divine nature, seeks to *embody* truth when unification of action and deed are identical, guided by the moral compass of conscience. Homo Divinitas emulates God when *embodying* Truth. The Lebanese poet Kahlil Gibran (1883-1931) leant another dimension to truth when he said, "I have no enemies oh God. But if I am to have an enemy, let his strength be equal to mine, that truth alone will be the victor."

Hereinafter, the word Truth will remain capitalized. In this divine context, the following concepts are presented as spiritual Truths:

First concept: Original Sin is myth; there is no *stain* of sin. Actions and words can be constructive or destructive, nurturing or hurtful, well intentioned or flawed, however the concept of sin is but an illusion, cyber-evil as it were. The consequences of the Garden of Eden, an event real or imaginary, are not ours to bear. To quote the nineteenth century British philosopher John Stuart Mill, "Over himself, over his own body and mind, the individual is sovereign." The illusion of sin has been propagated and made real by religions in order to usurp that sovereignty; to gain wealth, influence and power by offering salvation from the illusion they perpetuate. "The

Christian resolution to find the world ugly and bad has made the world ugly and bad." – Friedrich Nietzsche.

Second concept: Each human being is a creator. Human beings are capable of creating positive forces that promote wellness and happiness, and negative forces that manifest fear and harm. We cultivate the ramifications of who we are by how we conduct ourselves in the universe. If we unduly hurt or do harm to others, to the extent of that harm, we must accept the consequences of the negative karma we create. Karma: every action generates a force that returns to us that which we create. In other words, we reap what we sow. Conversely, to the extent we offer to ourselves and to others, kindness, understanding and forgiveness, so will the universe endow our actions with fulfillment and grace; if not in this life, then in the next.

Third concept: In the ecological quilt of all living things on this planet, *all life is sacrosanct*. Killing is meant for food sustenance *only*. In Buddhism, *ahimsa* is "putting away the killing of living things". Violence, whether physical or emotional, real or vicarious, demeans our divinity. Lethal violence against life is the ultimate spiritual blasphemy. Reasons deemed to be practical always can be found to *justify* killing. When considering actions within the arena of human events, these justifications may include self-defense, euthanasia, infanticide (killing of the unborn), capitol punishment, and murder under political immunity - war. Justifications for killing animals within nature's realm include killing animals for sport or trophy and instituting "kills" to balance an ecosystem we have caused to go out of balance. Indiscriminate harvesting of fish from the planet's oceans is naturally immoral. Practical justifications can be found for each of these cases nevertheless we must acknowledge from a moral perspective, that killing is the ultimate destructive act. Absolute sanctity of life is the paradigm that must be acknowledged and emulated.

Fourth concept: Prayers are best communicated through action. Hurt caused to others must be resolved by deeds not just words. Saying ten "Hail Mary's" is merely an emotional placebo. Prayer has its place however there are more appropriate prayers than selfish entreaties that begin with, "I want..." those are best directed to Santa. The truest prayer consists of two and only two words, "Thank you". "I have had prayers answered - most strangely so sometimes - but I think our heavenly Father's loving-kindness has been even more evident in what He has refused me." – Lewis Carroll.[a]

"Pointing to another world will never stop vice among us; shedding light over this world can alone help us." – Walt Whitman (1819-1892). Prayer is more effective when it becomes manifest in how we help our fellow man; spiritually it is just as important to be the answer to someone else's prayer, for they then may become the answer to our own. It could be said that our lives are a testament to the prayer we embody. Our lives are prayers in action. Every day can be a personal thank-you card written with the pen of reality on the parchment of life. Every day can be a renaissance of self-worth and appreciation for the abundance and richness of a *self-ordained* life of integrity and ethical veracity striving for behavioral maximums not plumbing societal minimums.

Fifth concept: The soul is eternal. Our genus regarding our present incarnation of spirit in human form is best referred to, not as Homo

---

[a] Charles Lutwidge Dodgson (1832-1898) better known as Lewis Carroll wrote *Alice's Adventures In Wonderland.*

sapiens (person of wisdom), but rather as *Homo Divinitas* (man of Divinity, or, man of Divine creation); divinity expressed in *human being*. Flora and fauna, as we currently experience them, do not dwell in the domain of ethics and morality at least to the extent we define them. Fauna kill however they do not create weaponry, they do not murder; nor do they war. Fauna have tenderness for their young however one seldom sees an animal stop in its tracks to behold a beautiful sunset. More than flora and fauna, Homo Divinitas inhabits a world of sophisticated choice not mere instinct. More than flora and fauna, Homo Divinitas is uniquely capable of *hope*. Hope is defined by Merriam-Webster as, "desire accompanied by expectation of fulfillment." Dictionary definitions are appropriately objective and factual and thus do not contain any element of poetry. The Scottish philosopher Thomas Carlyle (1795-1881) provided a more comprehensive definition of hope when he said, "Man is, properly speaking, based upon hope, he has no other possession but hope; this

world of his is emphatically the place of hope." Homo Divinitas is driven by the inertia of hope toward spiritual fulfillment.

These five concepts have one common theme that underscores and unites them - the miracle of life is an eternal blessing of the Divine Creator and each of us is an expression of Divinity. Secular profanity such as Darwin's evolution as applied to Homo sapiens or religious profanity such as Augustine's doctrine of "original sin" serve to obscure the innate endowment of goodness in Homo Divinitas.

CHAPTER 2
OUR PRACTICAL REALM

Charles Darwin (1809-1882) was an eminent scientist whose seminal work *Origin of Species* documented laws of "natural" selection and survival of the fittest. Science is the practice of applying intellect and reason to quantify, explain, and define, that which is finite, to measure that which is measurable. Mr. Darwin began from a **stained** premise when he included mankind in the "equations" of his theory. In the secular realm, Mr. Darwin seems to "ape" St. Augustine when he states, "We must, however, acknowledge as it seems to me, that a man with all his noble qualities...still bears in his bodily frame the *indelible* stamp of his *lowly* origin." (Italics added). This thought seems not to be isolated. Charles Darwin also commented, "The highest possible stage in moral culture is when we recognize that we ought to control our thoughts." Apparently the secular Mr. Darwin evolved little beyond his religious "brethren" Tertullian and Irenaeus. Though we have proceeded one generation past the postulation of "1984" envisioned and written by George Orwell it is not difficult to recognize the parallel between "Big Brother" of Orwell's prose and the mindsets of Messrs. Tertullian and Darwin.

One of Mr. Darwin's primary conclusions of natural law is that of "survival of the fittest". If mankind dwelled according to this principle, all of us by now would have 20-20 vision, detect approaching prey (criminals) at 1000 yards, and our "imperfect" young would perish at the behest of natural predators. Mankind is not in harmony with nature now, nor has he ever been. Under natural law, the science of medicine could not have developed in order to diminish or enhance nature's inertia. Contrary to natural law, we are unable to adapt to cold by developing thicker coats of hair or fur so the "naked ape" fashions clothes to insulate against cold weather.

Contrary to fauna of nature, human beings participate in cyber occult economic law, specifically those that govern laissez-faire capitalism, which is propelled by the inertia of profit. Profit is realized as resulting from the financial combustion arising from consumption qua production. Thus economic law, driven by the impetus of consumption, will always favor profit over nature, wealth over environment. Economic law (capitalism) compels mankind to develop disposable items thus creating mountains of non-biodegradable garbage because profit exists in doing so. Economic law will disfavor the wise who yearn for a return to natures blessings and reward the foolhardy who compromise nature for profit and sell their souls for money. "Capitalism has destroyed our belief in any effective power but that of self interest backed by force." – George Bernard Shaw (1856-1950). One might also add, the covert force of manipulation.

To the contrary, mankind creates disharmony with nature. Mankind synthesizes natural elements into non-biodegradable material, depletes the ozone layer, pollutes air with industrial emissions, contaminates the water table, befouls ocean and shore with oil, and commits animal sacrifice in the name of research (from medicine to mascara). Ann Coulter has said (not surprisingly), "God says 'Earth is yours. Take it. Rape it, it's yours.'[3] This remarkably candid observation reveals more about Ms. Coulter than Genesis 1:28! Her callous libido notwithstanding, Ms. Coulter had a like-minded predecessor in the person of James G. Watt, former Secretary of the Interior during the Reagan Administration (1981-1983). The Washington Post of May 24, 1981 quoted James Watt as saying, "We will mine more, we will drill more, cut more timber." And, "My responsibility is to follow the Scriptures which call upon us to occupy the land until Jesus returns." Not that Ms. Coulter or James Watt exemplify a majority view regarding the ecosystems of planet earth, nevertheless mankind, ipso facto, cannot dwell in the realm of nature as such cavalier attitudes and behavior contradict the laws of nature theorized by Mr. Darwin.

Life, as we experience life, is contained in two realms. Flora and fauna exist within the realm of nature. Mankind, which is to say Homo Divinitas, exists in a supra-natural realm. More than flora and fauna, Homo Divinitas is distinguished by a world of sophisticated choice wrought from knowledge within moral and ethical contexts as opposed to mere instinct. Nature maintains a law (or more appropriately, a force) of natural selection whereby nature exerts checks and balances through inter-specie inter-reaction. Every animal and/or plant is subject to a primary natural enemy and perhaps several secondary enemies. In fact the term "enemy" is too convenient. Human beings view and subsequently anthropomorphize animal behavior in terms congruent with human behavior. The term "enemy" falsely implies conscious adversarial conflict. However in nature's realm, any specie qua specie exists as a natural force that maintains balance in any given ecosystem. Life and death in the world of flora and fauna is an expression of mutual sustenance and existence qua environmental forces and weather. An ecosystem that exists in balance perpetuates in balance.

Nature's food chain is the primary structure that determines the establishment and maintenance of predator hierarchy and thus, ecological balance. Christianity has indoctrinated mankind with the assumption that all of nature is his "domain", ergo the inbred inertia for dominance. **Genesis 1:28**, "And God blessed them, and God said unto them, be fruitful, and multiply, and replenish the earth, and subdue it: and have dominion over the fish of the sea, and over the fowl of the air, and over every living thing that moveth upon the earth." Times, translations, bias, and etymology notwithstanding, might not God have said, or cause to have been transcribed, "Go forth in love and bear children in love. I have blessed you with Nature, treat Nature as you would Me. Share creation with others within creation and above all, revere and cherish life and love."

The exponential growth of mankind qua nature has been out of balance because mankind exists supra-naturally. Mankind of the supra-natural realm exists at the top of the food chain, therefore has no natural enemies (bacteria and viruses notwithstanding) other than *himself* to act as an agent of balance. Presently, population growth and its subsequent rabid consumption will, from an actuarial perspective, exponentially exceed man's capability to provide adequate sustenance (food and shelter) to an ever-increasing populace (for those fortunate enough to afford financial cost).

Population growth will overwhelm nature because, and in spite of, technology. Technology, as an extension of mankind, exponentially increases capacity for knowledge, research, and the communication of both, predictably careening forward under the masquerade of "progress". An automobile without brakes makes progress also. The Hindu term "dharma" refers to the underlying order in Nature and human life and behavior considered to be in accord with that order. Ethically, it means "right way of living" or "Proper Conduct," in the behavioral and moral sense. With respect to spirituality, dharma might be considered the Way of the Higher Truths. Hindus were far ahead of, and more comprehensive than Mr. Darwin when trying to understand life force.

Nature's metabolism has self-governing brakes such as "survival of the fittest" and "natural selection". God/Allah/the Great Integrity also gave mankind brakes in the form of Greater Law (morality and ethics, Higher Truth). Nevertheless Homo sapiens elects to ignore the brake pedal of discipline in lieu of the accelerator of consumption, exacerbated by the inertia of inflation and profit of occult Economic Law (free market capitalism). Technology is a cyber-projection, a tool of mind that extrudes a cyber-price (profit) from the Creation. Profit is thus offset by societies that have become sloth and obese with an undisciplined desire to do or consume. One of the four truths of Buddhism is that of samodaya, i.e. the perpetual thirst of the human spirit to be consuming. This consumption can be things, or experiences. Samodaya represents the tendency of human beings to take hold of their environment in dominion over it, and make it serve man, not the obverse. Samodaya may be the equivalent of spiritual diabetes.

Technology, as a manifestation of man, is a cyber-force without dimension, conscience, or awareness of Greater Law. Technology, as such, is a cyber-polemic that facilitates the worship of science, as opposed to the worship of creation or the Creator. Whereas with spiritual law aboriginal peoples honor and belong to land, conversely religious law (the book of Genesis 1:26) gives mankind ownership (dominion) of land. Technologies exist without being subject to predatory condition or influence nor are they subject to existential law. Technological inertia serves to facilitate efforts of Homo sapiens to transfuse the life blood of Nature into monetary profit by sapping her mineral and fossil wealth, over-harvesting bountiful foodstuffs from land and ocean with no constraints other than those limits of human gluttony. The English novelist Aldous Huxley (1894-1963) has observed, with reason, that at least environmentally, "Technological progress has merely provided us with more efficient means for going backwards."

Gluttony is manifest twofold, first with financial profit and yet again with conspicuous consumption. One myth regarding technology is that technology makes work easier. It does not. Technology makes work more productive, ergo more profitable, which causes more work. Like the proverbial dragon chasing its tail, technology drives productivity that drives profit, that funds research and development that drives more technology, that drives more work in an inexorable quest for profit. People who comprise the workforce now labor more than ever to sate the insatiable appetites of profit and dividend. Gluttony will eventually empty Nature's cupboard. The cyber (and occult) Law of Finance, i.e. that of supply and demand will insure prices such that only the wealthy will eat. Charity notwithstanding, the Law of Finance, in this case ruthless laissez-faire capitalism, will insure that profit will starve the poor and sate the rich.

Whether capitalism or socialism, laws of finance have nothing to do with nature though both systems are dominant predicates that influence and determine man's inter-reactions. Homo sapiens is adept at synthesizing research, material, marketing, and circumstance to optimize tangible financial profit. Homo sapiens however, is far less adroit when attempting to apply the same energy and determination to synthesize tolerance and understanding toward the intangible benefit of brotherhood. For centuries, peoples of society have necessarily been required to focus on financial profit in order to fund and secure their own needs and wants. Consequently the fulfilling grace and goodness of charity and sharing has been given short shrift. Peripherally, charity occurs but consider, how much charity is donated from the standpoint of tax write-off? Consider that eliminating financial profit (usury in all it's guises) from the equation of human inter-reaction would be tantamount to castrating the usurious financial rapists in our midst.

Usury in the vilest of guise is exercised in the arena of religious worship. Whereas, capitalism determines occult financial value[b] regarding the exchange of goods and services, whereas by definition, financial profit occurs upon any given commercial exchange, a consumer obtains, at cost (profit), a product or service. The product or service may be overpriced (usurious) however the consumer, wittingly or not, receives a tangible item. Organized religion, whether selling indulgences (stays of duration in purgatory) or salvation (a presence in heaven), has no production cost and for the most part operates in a tax-free environment. Yet organized religions accept tithes and monetary donations from those seeking that which they already possess, eternal life. Worshipers seek the "product" of salvation and/or peace of mind from the same religions that disturb the peace

---

[b] Agreed upon by society without any viable governance of value such as gold or silver.

by preaching fear, judgment, and vengeance. This author does not allege that pastors, preachers, imam's, or rabbi's interpret laity as dollar signs, but the enormous and systemic wealth and power of Organized Religion does belie altruistic intent.

Religious leaders do not interpret fellow believers as dollar signs or euros but government politicians do. Usury rears its head among those who govern not from tithe but through tax. The United States government usurps (taxes) when money is inert, i.e. savings and government receives a "rake" (commission) when money is dynamic, which is to say when it changes hands upon virtually every commercial interrelation between its citizens (sales tax). Taxation in all its manifestations is nothing more than state-sponsored legislation that authorizes usurious accumulation of wealth.

How debilitating and/or shallow it must be for an entrepreneur to perceive another person as a "$$", solely as an opportunity to sow a sale, garner a commission, only to reap profit? Alas, this mindset of the businessman differs no less in commercial and corporate environs and boardrooms. Quoting Charles Dickens (1812-1870), "Most men are individuals no longer so far as their business, its activities, or its moralities are concerned. They are not units but fractions."

Dickens realized this 150 years ago! Human Resources departments of businesses and corporations will mount campaigns of faux altruism to reassure employees that they are cared about, their safety is important, that workplace discrimination (racial, sexual, age, etc.) will not be tolerated, yadda yadda…but their concern goes only so far as *the minimum required by law*, compliance not empathy. Industrial and commercial decision-makers are concerned only with employee safety insofar as regarding workman's compensation and/or injury liability. If U.S. multi-national corporations and conglomerates (global ones too for that matter) cared about their citizens, jobs would not be outsourced to the lowest global pay-source, the U.S. manufacturing base would not be depleted, pension funds would not be plundered, stock options pre-dated, and illegal aliens courted in order to keep downward hydraulic pressure on the nations wage scale.

The United States abandoned the gold standard in 1971. In so doing, the government released economic value from the material constraint discipline of gold and silver and permitted the value of currency to float regulated only by the value people believed the dollar to possess. With no precious metal to govern currency values, financial wealth became an opportunity for investment as opposed to salary. The first generation to recognize and reap the rewards of that shift in policy realized that extraordinary wealth could be made from easy (though risky) investment as opposed to the hard work of wage-based jobs. Consequently baseball players and actors make millions of dollars and executive golden parachutes and stock options are valued to the obscene. By-and-large, any entry-level employee, supervisor, or manager for that matter, wants to be recognized and craves appreciation of performance but in many circumstances, financial influences overwhelm our better instincts, our caring hearts, and the workplace leaves us with thirst for acknowledgement and thanks that finance does not bequeath.

Samodaya is manifest in mankind's thirst to sate body because of neglect in nourishing the soul. The 21st century has witnessed the actuarial fury of consumption to satisfy physical desires and needs, conspicuous or essential, that is causing climate change, depletion of the ozone layer, accelerated melting of polar ice caps, massive deforestation, fauna extinction, and deadening of coral reefs. Samodaya in the realm of spirit is testimony to the failed attempts by established religions to provide fulfilling wholesome answers to the most complex of man's questions regarding his origin, destiny, and his infinity. For centuries, religions have indoctrinated civilizations with the premise that Divinity and the search therefore, must begin outside one's own self and be sanctioned and guided by the orthodox religious establishment. Ostensibly, organized religion served at cross-purpose with mankind's quest to know self and seek Divinity. This has empowered religious institutions at the expense of those who placed trust and fealty to those people and institutions that willingly usurped and manipulated the inertia of man's spiritual impetus and curiosity.

Thus, for centuries, people have been conditioned to search beyond and outside themselves when seeking the sovereignty of self-knowledge, self-identity, self-possession, spiritual direction and wholeness. Having conditioned the multitudes to externally search for eternal answers, religions have failed to adequately provide answers to address spiritual needs. Consequently, with the failure of religions to provide adequate spiritual enlightenment, the inertia of samodaya continues with the impulse of the external pursuit of drugs, and/or lifestyles that attempt to anesthetize the pain of unfulfilled spirituality. Incidentally, drugs come in many forms, not just those of pharmaceuticals. Drugs represent any addiction to a material source to quell inner anxiety or condition of malaise or trepidation. A "drug" which as yet, has not been recognized as such is a lifestyle that subliminally or consciously seeks and devours stress. Stress is a stimulant on which most of western society covets and craves. Ask the workaholic about stress. Ask yourself how really difficult it is and how long it takes to "unwind". Much like the tension of the inner springs of watches, tension, which is to say stress, is primarily determined by attachment to, and preoccupation with, the inexorable progression of the fixed rate of time.

Flora and fauna coexist not as neighbors so much as species governed by a greater law, that of natural balance, *iter natura* (nature's way). Whether butterfly or rhinoceros, each, within the confines of environment, perpetuate an ecosystem by being an integral part of it, by reacting to the unspoken forces of natural law. Mr. Darwin proposes "survival of the fittest" and "natural selection" however his "equations" fail to address intangibles. At natures calling, a beaver may construct a dam and a bird may build a nest, however animals do not have faith, do not have hope, and cannot give to charity. Eagles can fly however they cannot leave the atmosphere. A raccoon can take something but it is not theft. Hyenas can kill but they do not murder. An eagle is beautiful however Homo Divinitas *alone* expresses the beauty of the eagle in poetry.

Beavers will respond to instinct and work within natures calling to gnaw down or prune a tree in order to build a dam. However, the beaver does not ask why the dam must be built, why it must be built now, or complain that he is understaffed when building the dam. Spider or hippopotamus, dandelion or sequoia, all respond to, and obey, a calling greater than themselves for the mutual benefit of perpetuation of species, which is to say, the harmony of nature. The beaver can use only small trees that lie within the confines of his *natural* thus limited abilities. Mankind however, operating in the realm of knowledge and reason, has the ability to supersede nature in a super-natural way. Homo sapiens confront nature in a super-natural way when knowledge enables him (occasionally in defiance of reason) to create tools that overwhelm nature, even to her atomic core. Those super-natural tools may come in the form of a wheel or a saw, hydrocarbon spewing aerosols, or atomic and hydrogen bombs.

On a microcosmic level, the knowledge of how to create a saw, the ability to use one, and the desire of free will to disregard nature, can in two minutes fell a tree that took nature fifty years to grow. Still, on the microcosmic level, the same principle of easy death applies to mankind when considering that a madman can extinguish life with a bullet propelled by hate. Easy death is a path trod by cowards because it takes courage to survive, live, and thrive. Cowards do not possess courage, discipline, or honor, and ultimately victimize those whom they *envy*. On a macrocosmic level, we use tools of destruction on *ourselves*. The mind of man, having been fascinated by the sun has emulated and harnessed the power of the sun in the technology of his own bombs. One question, as yet unanswered, is whether or not mankind has wisdom and emotional wherewithal to keep from further using that power such as in Hiroshima and Nagasaki in 1945. A Greater Law too, governs Homo sapiens. More often than not, however mankind uses free will to disregard Greater Law and thus jeopardizes his own perpetuation. Quoting the founder of empiricist philosophy, John Locke (1632-1704), "Nature never makes things for mean or no uses." This jeopardy alone favors Mr. Locke and contradicts thus disproves Mr. Darwin.

Though mankind has attempted to harness disease caused by bacteria, mankind seems unable to vaccinate against hate, fear, and unmitigated violence. Human beings alone are capable of creating weapons to augment aggression. Homo sapiens alone is capable of homicide. Homo sapiens alone have developed a social ethos that allows, and conditionally *condones* state-sponsored (politically motivated) acts of multiple homicides - war. Homicide, the vilest of human deed, is an act that has been sponsored in the realm of religion such as the Crusades in the 11th century. Whence, "The aim of Christianity is not to fill the earth, but to fill heaven. Why should one worry if the number of Christians is lessened in the world by deaths endured for God? By this kind of death people make their way to heaven who perhaps would never reach it by another road."[4] This quote was gleaned from a report written by Humbert of Romans in the late 13th century. If one replaces "Christianity" with "Islam" and "Christians" with "Muslims" we have a situation that mirrors the events of our times.

Pope Benedict XVI delivered a speech at the University of Regensburg on September 12, 2006, that aroused controversy in the Islamic world when he quoted the late 14th century Professor Theodore Khoury, "Show me just what Mohammed brought that was new, and there you will find things only evil and inhuman. Such as his command to spread by the sword the faith he preached." Predictably the radical elements of the Islamic world acted no differently now than it did during the siege of Constantinople, essentially proving Pope Benedict's point. The following quote is from Pope Benedict's speech on which Islam chose not to focus, "The emperor, after having expressed himself so forcefully, goes on to explain in detail the reasons why spreading the faith through violence is something unreasonable. Violence is incompatible with the nature of God and the nature of the soul. "God", he says, "is not pleased by blood – and not acting reasonably is contrary to God's nature. Faith is born of the soul, not the body. Whoever would lead someone to faith needs the ability to speak well and to reason properly, without violence and threats... To convince a reasonable soul, one does not need a strong arm, or weapons of any kind. Or any other means of threatening a person with death."

One can only speculate why influential leaders of Islam would isolate the first comment out of context and for what reason? Wonder may also be directed at the congress of the United States when, at the bidding of the president, it recently chose to permit the United States government the capability to unilaterally interpret the hallowed Fourth Geneva Convention (GCIV Part 3, Section 1, Article 32) governing torture. Such actions are congruent with the terrorists we presume to be fighting. Radical Islam seems to be at war with a United States administration just as intent on its own terrorism.

"War is a mind-set. In certain cases, you may need to protect yourself or someone else from being harmed by another, but beware of making it your mission to "eradicate evil," as you are likely to turn into everything you are fighting against. Fighting unconsciousness will draw you into unconsciousness yourself. Unconsciousness, dysfunctional egoic behavior, can never be defeated by attacking it. Even if you defeat your opponent, the unconsciousness will simply have moved into you, or the opponent reappears in a new guise. Whatever you fight, you strengthen, and what you resist persists."[5] - Eckhart Tolle. This observation is tragically prophetic and in the case of the war initiated by the politicians of the United States against the government of the brutal Saddam Hussein, applies directly to the White House. Neo-conservatives or administration decision-makers are quite unaware of the philosophy of the late 19th century Russian writer Leo Tolstoy (1828-1910) who authored *The Kingdom of God Is Within You.* Quoting Tolstoy, "War on the other hand is such a terrible thing, that no man, especially a Christian man, has the right to assume the responsibility of starting it." Leo Tolstoy could not have anticipated the likes of George W. Bush, but the world might be a better place if "Dubya" had read Tolstoy while attending Yale University. Had "Dubya" read Tolstoy further; he would have found that "The greater the state, the more wrong and cruel its patriotism, and the greater is the sum of the suffering upon which it is founded."

Homo Divinitas (spiritual man) therefore must refocus our existence from being predatory to one of brotherhood, from violence and fear, to affection and forgiveness. Homo Divinitas must begin to realize the integrity and veracity of the Greater Law of ethics and morality. There is wisdom in sharing and selfishness in ownership. A better way of existence must be found. We must learn the courage of love and disdain the ego-driven weakness of predatorship. We must brake before the car crashes.

CHAPTER 3
OUR SPIRITUAL REALM

"Our greatest happiness does not depend on the condition of life in which change has placed us, but is always the result of a good conscience, good health, occupation, and freedom in all just pursuits."
– Thomas Jefferson.

Every human being (Homo Divinitas) is a divine expression of Divinity, the Great Integrity. Each and every being who has ever existed in all of eternity is *unique* by design and intent. Mathematics of the matter would seem to indicate that Divine intent and design must be so. Mathematical probabilities would compel duplication were it not for element of divine participation. When throwing two six-sided dice, the odds of duplication is one in six. The imaginary "odds" of having no duplication among billions of "dice" is incomprehensible. The defiance of this mathematical equation mandates design not chance. Max Planck won the Nobel Prize for Physics in 1917. With his acceptance speech he became one of the few scientists who transcended the chasm between faith and fact, "All matter originates and exists only by virtue of a force. We must assume behind this force the existence of a conscious and intelligent Mind. This Mind is the matrix of all matter."

Billions of human beings have lived and never have there been, nor are there now, nor will there ever be, any two persons alike. Twins may share a common genetic heritage however the souls who incarnate the bodies are *unique*, each an individual expression of Divine Creation. Souls pass from infinity through the finite and once again to infinity via the miracles of transition we refer to as conception and death. We are present in, and consequently more cognizant of, being in the realm of dimension because such is the state of our present awareness. It is interesting to note that sleep is an essential need that provides a respite from the continual exposure of the state of consciousness known as "reality". Within the confines of that present conscious awareness, everyone has a *unique* destiny. The most direct way to that destiny is being True to one's conscience. Taoism teaches, "The snow goose need not bathe to make itself white. Neither need you do anything but be yourself." – Lao Tse. A similar thought appears in the Talmud, "Every blade of grass has its Angel that bends over it and whispers, 'Grow, grow." Considering these statements, it takes courage to be true to one's self, to follow conscience to the greatest extent possible, and just as significantly, maintain the same integrity by acknowledging error when appropriate.

Mankind may be viewed more accurately from a perspective of spirit by considering the true gestation period of Homo Divinitas within dimensional existence. Gestation begins at conception and for the first nine months continues with in-utero incubation. Post-utero incubation consists of the socio-emotional-intellectual maturation/learning process, including though not limited to learning of practicalities of life, understanding consequences of choice, acquiring emotional and intellectual knowledge, awareness of spirituality, morals, and ethics. Growth continues though puberty, adulthood, and in a best-case scenario, is never-ending as we learn how to make, understand, and accept choices within those realms that can provide a basis for wholesome existence. Destiny looms for us much the same as it does for the white snow goose. To the extent we eliminate falsehood and pretense, to the extent we are honest with self and others, to the extent we refrain from judging others and self, we therefore have the opportunity and inclination to be able to refocus on, and enjoy the wonder of miracles that surround us.

This incarnation provides the miracle of experiencing reality as defined by four dimensions, five senses, and our own *unique* perspective with which to feel the consequences of choice within the miracle of the life-in-body dimensional experience. In a sense, the duality of being is such that simultaneously our bodies straddle the finite while our souls straddle infinity. Infinity is apparent to mankind because we are able to suppose and acknowledge that which is beyond our grasp of understanding. We are unable to comprehend the quantity of the largest number we can think of though we are aware that the largest number we can imagine is infinitely large. We have the ability to suppose there is more to life than finite fact and reason because we possess infinite faith and infinite belief, whether or not we elect to express them. Homo Divinitas is defined as a being of faith without limit, hope without limit, love without limit.

"Reason" as it pertains to human endeavor is a governing influence that determines whether behavioral motivation is constructive or destructive, whether actions and/or words have "good" reasons or "bad" reasons. "Reason", in the realm of applied science is manifested by postulations and theory regarding the contemporary perspective of the measurable universe; to the extent those measures can be accepted as accurate. Quoting Thomas Paine, "Every science has for its basis a system of principles as fixed and unalterable as those by which the universe is regulated and governed. Man cannot make principles; he can only discover them." Science is committed to discovery of fact and postulation through research and logic. The capacity of reason ends where dimensions, i.e. time and space, end. "Reason" may extend beyond that which is finite however the extrapolation of reason beyond the bounds of dimension is merely an influence of speculation.

That being the case, "I do not feel obliged to believe that the same God who has empowered us with sense, reason, and intellect, has intended us to forego their use." – Galileo Galilei (1564-1642). One may also wish to consider that faith begins where reason ends. Faith is the act of emotional concordance that something unsubstantiated by fact is real. Faith is that element of creation that permits Homo Divinitas to transcend the limits of fact and logic. One of Galileo's contemporaries, the English poet John Donne (1572-1631) provides the perfect compliment to Galileo with the following thought, "Reason is our soul's left hand, faith her right." Thomas Carlyle echoed Donne two hundred fifty years later; "Imagination is a poor matter when it has to part company with understanding." Faith, hope, and love represent the domain of the poet while the scientist provides a definition of factual backdrop as a stage for the appassionata of life. Science has discovered DNA and brought us to the threshold of space exploration but the Poet created the divine up reach within Homo Divinitas to discover the building blocks of life and to extend the impetus of creation to reach for the stars…and to love our brothers and sisters. Put quite simply, "Love takes up where knowledge leaves off", Saint Thomas Aquinas.

Just as "Truth" was defined earlier, the word "believe" will now be defined for use in the text. Merriam-Webster defines the term "believe" as: 1) to have religious conviction (sic!), 2) to have firm conviction about something: accept as true, 3) to hold as opinion. This author has a more compelling definition of the term "believe". The prefix 'be' is understood to enable or facilitate the verb or noun it modifies. Consider the following words, beget, belie, bemoan, belabor, befuddle, begrudge, beguile, beset, *because*. To *believe* is to *be-life* – to give life and being to thought, to make live, to make *real*. Belief is powerful when one considers the context just proposed. "Believe" or "belief" has more gravitas than suppose or supposition, assume or assumption. Belief has no contamination of doubt. Therefore the true etymology of the term "become" or "became" is belief made real. Evidence of this is the Buddhist statement, "in the sky, there is no distinction of east and west; people create distinctions out of their own minds and then *believe* them to be true." (Italics added). Action, when applied to belief causes events to transform from possibility into occurrence. Discipline and determination, or lack thereof, cause events and thereby determine the quality of the inheritance of our individual and collective destinies.

The fullest extent of the exercise of reason *and* faith add richness to the human experience. Children possess unlimited faith, hope, and love, however with the aging process, adults tend to program themselves to *believe* that limits to faith, hope, and love do exist. Limits are adopted from interpretations of external sources and are not natural – an infant is incapable of hate. Emotional limits are learned from and bestowed by those who, having had no choice other than to accept limits from their forebears, pass them on to their progeny. As toddlers and young children, we do not question the force of opinion or reason, of our peers, elders, and parents because we have not had the opportunity to scrutinize experiences of life through the lens of learned choice.

Toddlers and young children are so innocent and emotionally defenseless they accept that which *is*, as opposed to that which *should* or *could be*. Tragically, the innocence of their world is no match for the influence and power of adult practicality. Ironically, external forces of opinion and bias are not correct, so we learn and thus are programmed with incorrect interpretations of being. It is said that adults use 3-7% of their brains, yet adults presume to teach children how to be. A story is told of a young child in a playroom who invariably creates a mess. Yes, the child has *created* something, but only adults call it a mess! The "mess" is in the adult mind! Ideally, the child is permitted to *create* a mess, and then to *create* order, and in the process, appreciate the *art* of *creation*. "Every child is an artist. The problem is how to remain an artist once he grows up." – Pablo Picasso.

Children, teens and adults, progressively leave the wisdom of innocence behind as they are forced to reduce recollections of infinity to finite definitions represented by mere vocabulary of verbal language. Ironically, it may be that we could learn the wisdom of infinity from a "new-born" in tune with the entirety of the brain that has not been programmed to neglect the 93-97%! Indeed, all have heard the phrase, "out of the mouths of babes". Aldous Huxley has said, "A child-like man is not a man whose development has been arrested; on the contrary, he is a man who has given himself a chance of continuing to develop long after most adults have muffled themselves in the cocoon of middle-aged habit and convention." Huxley also said "we are all geniuses up till the age of ten." The

Danish philosopher Soren Kierkegaard (1813-1855) said, "Life can only be understood backwards but it must be lived forwards." How intellectually tantalizing it is to consider a type of reverse scenario whereby stoic, critical, aged adults could proceed toward the innocence of youth! Indeed, that scenario is real and can be recognized once the case for reincarnation is acknowledged.

Youthful innocence assumes reason to be untainted by *motive* because innocence is unaware of malice. Maturity affords the opportunity to differentiate opinion, realize distinctions, and determine faultless or faulty reasoning and/or motive. Occasionally opinion masquerades as reason and opinions are seldom neutral or non-causal. Children unavoidably confuse contaminated opinion with fact or what is considered "good" reason because they know no better. Maturity can offer the opportunity to enable our selves to break the chains of opinion and tainted motive, and in so doing, recreate an unlimited horizon of possibilities and emotional freedom. "The great man is he who does not lose his child-heart. He does not think beforehand that his words shall be sincere, nor that his acts shall be resolute; he simply abides in the right." – Chinese philosopher Mencius (371 B.C. – 289 B.C.).

Harkening back to the child-heart of which Mencius speaks, remember back to childhood and the absolute wonder and joy we felt about a man who lived at the North Pole named Santa Claus? The power of belief is enormous. And please consider that "power" in this case is a misnomer. Though "power" can refer to strength or intensity of force, in this particular case, "power" is best understood as the extent of the capacity for possibilities. Virtually anything is possible for children until they are dissuaded by people (who have not tried or succeeded) that they cannot. For millions of persons who once believed in Santa Claus, the world of wonder of such belief was spectacular and joyous. Because we believed in Santa Clause, we realized him, *made him real*, if only to our selves. Opportunities for joy and wonder occur only if and when possibilities exist. To the extent possibilities do not occur, opportunities do not exist. This is not to say that adults should believe in Santa Claus, however adults need to believe in possibilities. Maturity confers wisdom on those people who have the courage to develop the traits of understanding, forgiveness, and knowledge of, and empathy for, the human condition. For those who elect not to walk the path of courage, karma will provide yet another opportunity for gnosis, enlightenment, a better way, via another incarnation.

Quoting Oprah Winfrey, "What I learned at a very young age was that I was responsible for my life. And as I became more spiritually conscious, I learned that we are responsible for our selves, that you create your own reality by the way you think and therefore act. You cannot blame apartheid, your parents, your circumstances, because you are not your circumstances you are your possibilities."[6] Limits, unknowingly self-applied during youth, may be knowingly self-removed with the wisdom of age. Do not say they cannot. The shackled are those who to a great extent permit their own shackles.

With much less fanfare than that which would accompany Oprah Winfrey, a courageous man named Nganga Maruge made the courageous choice to throw off his shackles. In the Los Angeles Times of February 6, 2005, Robyn Dixon reported the story of Nganga Maruge, dateline Kasarani, Kenya. At 85 years of age this man who had never received any schooling of any sort, decided he wanted to attend primary school so he could learn to read and write. He had to sell a sheep to buy a uniform and black shoes. He told Jane

Obinchu, the school Principle, that "he wanted to learn so he could read the Bible." Quoting the Los Angeles Times article, Mr. Mruge is "a widower who was jailed for eight years by Kenya's former British rulers for his Mau Mau anticolonial activities, Maruge lives alone in a cluttered wooden hut. There is one window, and a 1944 bicycle is propped to one side. His school uniform is slung over a stool, and his school tie and bag hang on the end of the bed." Incredibly some parents of children in the class which Mr. Maruge attends are resentful of the attention he receives, seemingly at the detriment of their own children. When this article was written there was a movement underway to have Mr. Maruge transferred from class and to transfer the Principal. "Maruge says his neighbors have hurt his feelings and he has few friends left. He just has his homework and his Kiswahili Bible, which he can't read yet." Throughout the controversy Dixon quotes Mr. Maruge as saying, "I feel lonely but I think it's good for me," he said. "I'm very happy in my heart. Now I know about writing, and I can add one plus one. I can read my name, and if it's a name like Grace, I can read Grace. I can write all the names of things like snake and leopard." Further Dixon quotes the Principal, "But even if he does not make it, he has been an inspiration to the whole world. Inside himself he can say, 'I went to school like everybody else.' That thirst for education will be quenched." Not only does Ngange Maruge recognize the name Grace, he knows more of grace than most of us will ever know.

One of the most enabling traits one can develop is that of self-esteem because self-esteem opens doors for those who have the courage to open them. Self-esteem overcomes pity. Self-esteem deigns selfishness. Self-esteem seeks to nourish others. Significantly, the artistry of a caress or of understanding for a loved one can help to shape and nurture our fellow living sculptures in Divinity's creation. In order to apply that artistry we must first learn the technique of self-application. It may well be a metaphysical standard to state that the capacity to love another person is no greater than one's own capacity to love one's self. That is not a statement of conceit. It is however an understanding that to more fully love someone else, we should first love ourselves. In so loving ourselves, we can then share that love more fully with some one else. Self-esteem must be experienced so it can be shared with those whom we wish to love more fully. "If you want to be respected by others the great thing is to respect yourself. Only by that, only by self-respect will you compel others to respect you." – Fyodor Dostoevsky (1821-1881)."

A remarkable book was published in 2006 entitled *Buddy Booby's Birthmark*, the book was written by a young boy, Evan Ducker, and his mother Donna. Evan was born with a hemangioma, a red port wine stain birthmark on his face. Quoting from Hannah Storm's Foreword to the book, "I was born with a vascular birthmark under my left eye. Without makeup, I look exactly like someone who has been in a fistfight! I constantly receive comments about my 'black eye' as an adult…And as a child I was extremely self-conscious. However my parents instilled in me a great sense of self-confidence… a 'follow your dreams' attitude that carried me into the appearance-conscious world of television, despite my 'imperfection'. My mother always told me when I was younger that my birthmark was on the place on my face that the 'angel kissed me' before she gently set me down upon this earth. However romantic that notion, I have always clung to it, for I do feel blessed and special…blessed with a loving family and talents that no birthmark can blemish."[7]

Quoting from Evan's mom in her Note to Parents, Physicians, Educators, and Caregivers, "On the Fourth of July, 1994, my husband Greg and I gave birth to our only child Evan. He was healthy and handsome with huge brown eyes, dimples, and a red port wine stain on his face. To us, a birthmark was not a big deal. However, we would soon find out, for *a lot* of other people—it was a really big deal. No one could have prepared us for what lay ahead. Like a magnet, Evan's birthmark seemed to attract every ignorant, insensitive person within a one-mile radius. Virtually everyone was compelled to walk up to us and pass a comment. It wasn't always *what* was said, but *how* it was said. If we had a dollar for every time someone asked' "What's **wrong** with his face?" I believe we could end world hunger. Strangers also freely shared their theories of how Evan got his birthmark – which ran the gamut from my 'wishing for wine during pregnancy' to 'being burned by fire in another life.' Just when I thought it couldn't get any worse – someone would give me a suspicious look or actually accuse me of child abuse! I was amazed by how little people knew about birthmarks, even doctors. Then one day at the age of four, Evan innocently asked why none of his books had characters with bookmarks. After taking a trip to the library, we discovered there weren't any. Sensing my son's disappointment, I casually said we could write our own story. Buddy Booby was born! While giving me all his imaginative ideas for the book, Evan decided the main character Buddy should be granted a wish. In my superior adult mind, I *KNEW* my son would have Buddy wish for his birthmark to go away. After all, it would make his life easier, (and would have been my choice if the situation were reversed). Imagine how foolish I felt when my little boy said, 'Why would Buddy wish for a dumb thing like that?' At that exact moment, I was overwhelmed by my son's compassion, selflessness, and wisdom.

Despite the treatment he received from many others, Evan had no bitterness and held no grudges. He had no desire to change, and he was not concerned about making life 'easier' for himself. Evan knew what mattered and nobody else's opinion could change that. I knew I had to share his extraordinary story."[8]

Their inspirational love toward Evan is expressed without influence from evolutionist theory or religious dogma. Though, in all honesty, Mr. Darwin, Christianity, and Islam are not the only myths that contaminate the self-image of Homo Divinitas. North African (Sudanese) myth speaks of Ajok, creator of the Universe, who (predictably) made mankind in his own image. When the child of the first pair of humans died, the mother prayed to Ajok to give life back to the child. Ajok did grant her wish and was about to grant the child and all subsequent descendants immortality when the child's father angrily interrupted. Furious that he had not been consulted, the man killed both child and mother. Ajok, (predictably) behaved much like "our" God and with petulance and spite left the earth in a snit leaving mankind to be plagued by death to this very day. In Uganda, babies born with a cleft are given the name "Ajok" which literally means "cursed by God".

Evan's parents (and those of Hannah Storm) were angels when they blessed their children with self-esteem and a sense of inner beauty. One can merely wonder how Homo Divinitas would thrive if we could all share in abundances of kindness and understanding not the 'birthmark' of original sin.

Youngsters prior to attaining awareness of self-esteem, develop sense of identity from actions and reactions of people who inhabit intimate space. Readers who have young ones in their lives may wish to keep in mind the following anonymously written poem:

How Do I Learn Just Who I Am

I learn from you who I am.
Within your eyes I see
    reflected me.
Within your voice, I hear
      how you see me.
You are the mirror that I look into
    And mold the image of myself.
I sense the way you hold me,
      And from your touch
          I feel my form, my shape.
And if I like what I see in
    Your eyes,
        Your voice,
           Your touch—
My heart responds and reaches out.
Then in it's reaching, grows and grows,
    Until I see myself as separate.
That separate self, in turn,
    Can love you back.
Because you taught me who I am,
    And I am loved.

This poem is just as appropriate in considering behavior with peers and elders as with children. No one is ever so old as not to be privileged to be able to hear one more compliment. No one can ever be so calloused as not to be able to feel the tenderness of one more caress just one more time.

The twentieth century Spanish artist Pablo Picasso (1881-1973) was quoted as saying, "My mother said to me, 'If you are a soldier, you will become a general. If you are a monk, you will become the Pope.' Instead, I was a painter and became Picasso." Picasso's mother had the loving emotional awareness to instill confidence and self-esteem in her child so he would excel in any endeavor. His blessing, as it were, was to be able to express his brilliance in the way of his own choosing. Brilliance is best expressed without the fetters of outside interference.

There is more emotional wellness in the above passages and in *Buddy Booby's Birthmark* than in the Old Testament, Book of Revelation, or Qu'ran, or other North African mythology. Verily, each of the formal religious texts could begin and end with one verse. "Do unto others as you would have them, do unto you." That is perhaps an overstatement but essentially, when trying to comprehend the magnificence of creation, it is indeed difficult, yea unfathomable to conceive of the great Integrity as a persona possessed by wrath, vengeance, and power lust. "Believe in me or go to hell" are not the words of a loving Divinity. From the Qu'ran we read (Surah IX, verse 68) Allah promiseth the hypocrites, both men and women, and the disbelievers fire of hell for their abode. It will suffice them. Allah curseth them, and theirs is lasting torment."

These spiritual travesties, whether from the Bible or Qu'ran, were written by self-serving, power-grubbing, insecure thought-despots whose words have cast millions of souls into the chaos of neurosis and self-denial. That aside, consider the following excerpt from the book *Pilgrim at Tinker Creek* by Annie Dillard, "Eskimo: If I did not know about God and sin, would I go to hell?" Priest: "No, not if you didn't know". Eskimo: Then why did you tell me?" Incidentally, a priest familiar with Gnostic Gospels would probably *not* quote the following scripture to that same Eskimo, "The Savior said there is no sin, but it is you who make sin when you do the things that are like the nature of adultery, which is called sin." - Gospel of Mary (4:26). That, simply put, would not be good <u>business</u>.

Referencing the earlier quote from Eckart Tolle, one may well posit that religion has caused the sin it professes to combat, thereby justifying the need of its own existence. Conceivably, conflict, spiritual paranoia, and the resultant emotional friction existent in spiritus mundi (the human condition, our collective world ethos) of today's world is caused by organized religion whose concept of "sin" represents a schizophrenic expression of the spirituality of mankind. Perhaps religion, as such, represents the egoic expression of mankind's spiritual identity in which our self-image has become that of Homo sapiens, a stained, unworthy, yet salvageable creation.

Stained religious thought such as "original sin" and stained secular theory such as man's evolution from animal must be replaced with unstained, non-dogmatic self-expression of spirit and the unfettering of the natural impulse to unify with Divinity. In so doing, people may then express above all else, understanding, tenderness, forgiveness, love of self, and love for those who constitute the entire tapestry of the creation of life. In so doing, the self-image realized will render that of Homo Divinitas. Homo Divinitas will thrive when "salvation" and evolution are recognized as nonsense. Homo Divinitas will flourish when we realize the destiny of the human family is to a great extent, wrought by our own efforts, and when we realize that eternal life is our divine birthright.

The gift of life and the gift of the afterlife are the two greatest gifts from the Divine Source available to all of Homo Divinitas. Indeed each consists of the other. "The day which we fear as our last is but the birthday of infinity." – Seneca (5 B.C. – 65 A.D.). The paradise of Eden, Nirvana apotheosis, or enlightenment, does not require brokerage fees from spiritual leeches that inhabit organized religion. This is not to say that religious officials and theologians are parasites, it goes without saying they are not. However, those who hide behind false doctrine or dogma, or defame by action, oaths they have vowed to uphold, and subsequently deny doing so, are the leeches referred to herein. "Hypocrisy is the homage vice pays to virtue." – Francois de la Rochefoucauld (1613-1680). Hypocrisy by deed or word is spiritual perjury. All persons are capable of error or misdeed. All too, are capable of admitting misdeeds, atoning for them, and beginning afresh.

Our spiritual imprint on destiny is defined by how we treat our selves and each other. We develop the "language" of spiritual expression through experiences of childhood and our exposure to, and how we interpret, formal creeds, philosophies, and religious thought during puberty and adulthood. For whatever cause, if we are unable to summon the emotional courage or emotional discipline to believe, or if we become unaware, or discontinue to realize unlimited love and unlimited possibilities, it is as though they do not exist. **They do exist**. We need just to realize them, i.e. to make them real. That is where the divinity of humanity (Homo Divinitas) enters the equation. We have faith, we have hope, and we have the courage, should we choose to express it, to regain love, to regain freedom, to establish and embrace self-esteem through the discipline of actions congruent with principle, wholesome values, and sound ethical behavior. Uncommon courage of common people arises in times of crises. Perhaps now is the time to begin exerting courage without waiting for the catalyst of crises. A random act of courage may be the act of apology, it may be an anonymous donation, it may be pulling a punch and it may constitute withholding an insult. Courage is not just saving a life. Courage, however and whenever it is expressed, enhances the quality and fullness of life. Courage may best be described as facing one's own worst negative prejudice, and finding out that in so doing, one may eliminate the cancer that resided *within* one's own self.

Life and the pursuit of happiness and/or fulfillment can be best expressed in the ancient Greek term "arete` (pronounced *ar-uh-tay*)". Arete` was defined as the process of striving to reach and realizing ones highest potential. It was Socrates himself who embodied this creed, "It is not living which is important, but living rightly." The road of virtue is more difficult than the road of expediency. The path of honor and honesty will more often than not, lead to spiritual richness not necessarily material riches.

So the die is cast for people of honor to choose the difficult way. Much as the salmon swimming against the current to earn the right to spawn newborn, the struggle to maintain honorable conduct is just as intense. However, nature's law of selection is not the arbiter of survival so much as the determination and steadfastness of the most virtuous of men and women. This can be a daunting exercise. The Japanese have a saying that says, in paraphrase, "The nail that stands up tends to get hammered down." This concept was known too in the nineteenth century. Quoting French author Victor Hugo (1802-1885), "Society is a republic. When an individual tries to lift themselves above others, they are dragged down by the mass, either by ridicule or slander." Whether or not this is still the case (and a strong case can be made that it is), genuine leaders must be able to withstand the courage of their convictions. Withstanding the crucible of dialectic, thought-smiths are able to produce ideas strong enough to withstand ridicule and slander in order to endure as signposts for future generations.

Ridicule and slander in today's religi-political world is manifested in its most extreme form as terrorism. Much of the planet is awash with conflict and terror between the more radical elements of Islam and, for lack of a better term, Judeo-Christianity, i.e. the "west". While the "west" has established forms of government predicated on direct election of representatives, it has also produced an environment whose culture is immersed in violence and sex. Radical Islam uses this cultural context to justify its war against the Great Satan. A compelling case can be made that such aggression is driven by jealousy. If the "west" with its faults were not so attractive, Islam would not be driven to attack that which it envies. "Decadence is a difficult word to use since it has become little more than a term of abuse applied by critics to anything they do not yet understand or which seems to differ from their moral concepts." – Ernest Hemingway (1899-1961).

Interpretations of reality are filtered by one's own state-of-mind. Both Qu'ran and Bible contain threats and violence however they only become relevant when a violent person identifies with religiously sanctioned threats and violence. Depending on the mindset of the person, a steak knife is harmless when cutting steak or lethal when used as a weapon. Steak knife, the Internet, religious text, a pencil or pen, may be either beneficial or malevolent depending on the mind and motive of the user. Life provides tools at our disposal that we may create art or despair, happiness or conflict. Those who terrorize, those who hurt and harm, may wish to reconsider their own state of mind. Most assuredly the negativity they perpetuate is a reflection of them selves. Most certainly the dysfunctionality of the terrorist is evident by his own self-condemning actions and perceptions.

Quoting Buddhist thought, "It is a man's own mind, not his enemy or foe, that lures him to evil ways." One may consider whether or not Seneca was familiar with Buddhism but he was as eloquent as Buddha when he said, "Whatever one of us blames in another, each one will find in his own heart." Two thousand years later, Nobel Prize winning author, Hermann Hesse echoed the wisdom of his predecessors when he said, "If you hate a person, you hate something in him that is a part of yourself. What isn't part of ourselves doesn't disturb us." In the greater scheme of the spiritual ethos of creation, the terrorist will be condemned by his own hand, by his own hatred.

Terrorism, incidentally, is not a new strategy or concept. Terrorism in other guise has existed since societies began to coalesce. Prior to the extended conflict in the Middle East or Ireland when the term came into vogue, people who used force or violence to coerce were simply referred to as common bullies. Terrorists are nothing more than glorified bullies on the steroid of religious fervor. A terrorist-cum-bully simply put, is one whose brain is smaller than his fist. Quoting philosopher John Dewey (1859-1952), "What is sometimes called an act of self-expression might better be termed one of self-exposure; it discloses character – or lack of character – to others." Bullies have not the mental means or stamina to reason in any sophisticated manner and consequently are unable or unwilling to accept the moral and ethical consequences of their myopic actions. The bully in the schoolyard, workplace, Gaza, or manipulative relationship must resort to intimidation, fear, and stealth because he lacks the acumen, ability to reason, and emotional maturity to recognize, consider, or accept views other than his own selfish motivation, be it a candy bar, a promotion, or martyrdom. Bullies react only to those basic reflexive instincts common to the animal world. Quoting the 19th century German philosopher Arthur Schopenhauer whose wisdom predates current religi-bombers, "Martyrdom is the only way a man can become famous without ability".

Terrorists, Jihadists, or Christian crusaders, of any century, are not lambs of God but rather wolves in sheep's clothing propelled by dogma and intolerance endemic to religi-fanaticism. George Bernard Shaw once said, "Hatred is the cowards revenge for being intimidated." The wisdom of Shaw, Schopenhauer, and the *patience* of legions of wise and like-minded astute individuals will provide testimony to the futility and impotence of the religi-fad of suicidal martyrdom. Patience is a significant quality that has far more dimension than knowing how to wait in a long line. Patience is the capacity to accept delay, adversity, or suffering without becoming angry or upset. Tolerance is the first cousin of patience.

"Justification" is the gate crasher to the house of patience and tolerance. Justification is a self-authored permission slip that authorizes any behavior and validates any action. Spiritually and morally, homicide is never justifiable but legally, courts of law recognize this defense. Most often, a "higher cause" is leveraged to justify retaliations that are otherwise, unjustifiable. More often than not, righteous (in a religious context) indignation is a catalyst that leads to outrageous indignation, accusation and vindictiveness. More than initial outrage, the more severe the vindictiveness, the more severe the punishment. In Latin, the term "vindicta" meant deliverance, revenge, or punishment. A vindicta was a rod used to discipline a slave. Vindictiveness acts like a quagmire; it sucks in those who come in contact with it. Vindictiveness reaches a nadir when manifested in the form of religi-bomber martyrdom.

It is interesting, at this point, to note the etymology of the word "martyr". "Martyr" had its origin in the Old English *martir*, via ecclesiastical Latin from the Greek *martur*, to "witness". Religious doctrinaires and thought-police have warped the definition of "heresy" into thought-crime and the definition of "witness" into sanctioned entrance to heaven, or by the extermination of infidels, entrance to Jannat (Islamic heaven).

Freedom will always conquer repression, it always has. Throughout centuries, the Caesars and the Attilas, the Hitlers and Stalins, the Maos and Czars have never prevailed because of the vacuum of any moral component in their doctrine. Similarly, doctrine of any religion, weak in spiritual gravitas will ultimately fail if its conveyance needs the enforcement of a strong fist because fists never prevail. Better to duel with ideas than pistols, but the unlearned or unintelligent have not ideas so they resort to dogma, pistols or individual-explosive-devices. The intellectual thugs of radical Islam would better serve Islam if they chose a war of words but as yet, no debate has been proposed. Fanatics of radical Islam choose to fight with bullets and bombs. Such is the case because quite apparently, they lack the intellectual veracity to advocate their cause in the arena of intellect and reason. The actions of the religi-bombers and terrorists bear testimony to the impotence of their spirituality and lies at the farthest fringe of the testimony of Muhammad the prophet. If Islam had moral or spiritual presence, Allah would not need "soldiers" to enforce policy any more than Christian soldiers marching ever onward. Policies of suppression or domination and/or the people who espouse them, whether originating from David Koresh, Jim Jones, Jerry Falwell, Pat Robertson, Benny Hinn, Robert Schuler, Ayatollah Khomeini, Hezbollah, are fraught with repression and religi-paranoia, thus are doomed to fail before they begin. The Vatican notwithstanding, history has never witnessed a successful self-perpetuating theocratic state. That said, if the United States foreign policy is one that espouses democracy as an expression of it's own people, the United States should endorse a Sunni, or Shiite state in the Middle East just as it does for the Jewish population of Israel.

CHAPTER 4
ARTISTIC EXPRESSION

"All art is autobiographical. The pearl is the oyster's autobiography."
– Federico Fellini.

"For once you have tasted flight, you will walk the earth with your eyes turned skywards, for there you have been and there you will long to return"
– Leonardo da Vinci.

Art is flight and flight is art. The artistic impulse of Homo Divinitas is unparalleled in nature. Flora and fauna do not dwell in the domain of ethics and morality at least to the extent we define them. A spider may construct a web, a beaver a dam, a bee a hive, and each are beautiful. In fact however, the structures of the animal kingdom are constructed to be practical and functional. Beauty lies not in these structures themselves so much as in *our* interpretations of them. No animal can sculpt a Pieta, play the piano, or compose a symphony. The Supreme Being created the planets however composer Gustav Holst provided humanity with their soundtrack.

The spider in its own beautiful way with its own innate degree in structural engineering will weave its web in order to gain sustenance. Nature is in perfect harmony, yet nature's perfection is a matter of expression, specie qua specie. Homo Divinitas responds to the artistic/creative urge in such a way as to express divine upreach so to *share* with other Homo Divinitae. A spider will not build a web for another spider that is infirm. A beaver will not ask other beavers how beautiful is his dam. Homo Divinitas is blessed to be able to express creativity at a Divine level.

Aldous Huxley said of music, "After silence, that which comes nearest to expressing the inexpressible is music." Music is subject neither to political geo-boundary nor the limitations of cumbersome vocabulary. The brilliant pianist Peter Donohoe made the following statement during the 1982 Tchaikovsky Competition in Moscow; "If it is said that one nationality of performer does not understand the music of another nationality...I think that is a very destructive thing. Russian music is central to the pianist's repertoire. Particularly, nineteenth century Russian music has a certain virtuosity, which is quite unparalleled in other nationalities. It's very, very important for the pianist to understand Tchaikovsky and Rachmaninoff. To imagine that Russians are the only people who can really see through it is actually, I think, a big mistake and I don't think Tchaikovsky or Rachmaninoff would thank anybody for that."[c] When creativity is expressed in the field of music, many would suggest Ludwig van Beethoven attained the highest level of expression. "Art! Who comprehends her? With whom can one consult concerning this great Goddess? – Ludwig van Beethoven. Elisabeth Brentano attended a party hosted by her father, Franz Brentano, a prosperous merchant and patron of the arts. One of the attendees at this party

---

[c] Politics polluted the competition when prizes were awarded. In the piano competition, remarkably, no first prize was awarded. Mr. Donohoe shared second prize with a gifted Russian, Vladimir Ovchinikov. Mr Donohoe has with time received the "first prize" from those of the music world who continually acknowledge his virtuosity.

was none other than Ludwig van Beethoven. "On May 28, 1810, she wrote enthusiastically about him to Goethe, whom she knew not merely through neighborly relations with his family in Frankfurt, but through a visit with him in Weimar. Some excerpts from this famous letter: When I saw him of whom I shall now speak to you, I forgot the whole world. ...It is Beethoven of whom I now wish to tell you, and who made me forget the world and you. ... He himself said. "When I open my eyes I must sigh, for what I see is contrary to my religion, and I must despise the world which does not know that music is a higher revelation than wisdom and philosophy, the wine which inspires one to new generative processes, and I am the Bacchus who presses out this glorious wine for mankind and makes them spiritually drunken."[9]

In an age of political correctness this final line may not land with the reader as it would have in contemporary 19th century Germany yet his passion is clear and his music has remained and always will be immortal, a reflection of his soul. As one listens to the 5th, 7th, and 9th Symphonies of Beethoven one wonders how a mortal human being (homo sapiens) can conceive and create such profound and overwhelming beauty. Yet, there is an answer to that question. The answer is that Beethoven's body was *mortal* yet his mind/soul is *immortal*. He was blessed to be able to create such works, and we are no less blessed to be able to enjoy them. Art and life imitate each other and neither is intended to be a solo journey. The same parallel exists in a sensory context with the hypothetical tree that fell in a forest. If one could not hear Beethoven's 9th Symphony, would it exist? Revisiting Augustine in a spiritual context, if there is no mind to perceive Truth, would Truth exist? The answer is yes, however it becomes art when the magnificence of Beethoven's music or

Divinity's creation is *shared*. "There are two ways of spreading light: to be the candle or the mirror that reflects it." – Edith Wharton.

The Merriam-Webster Dictionary (1974) defines art as, "The use of skill and imagination in the production of things of beauty." A more poetic definition of art has been provided by Michelangelo, "A true work of art is but a shadow of divine perfection." In the beginning of the 21st century, difficulty lies in attempting to ascertain whether art, as such, has maintained an impetus of production toward the goal of beauty. As discussed in *Rosebud*[d], faux power is the control of other people as opposed to the genuine power of self-control. Ersatz art, as it relates to the world of creativity, resorts to shock, vulgarity, and disgust. True artistic intent creates beauty and inspiration. The expression of faux art is similar to the insecure and immature child who, upon learning a new word of profanity, keeps using the word to gain attention. Expressions of profanity, violence, or depravity debase the concept of artistic expression to which the "artist" seemingly aspires. Naming examples of contemporary individuals who abuse their medium of expression would serve only to further bestow a measure of notoriety on those who seek it, where none is due. The most egregious offenders are readily apparent. Their self-image is apparent too in how they conduct themselves and how they wish to be identified.

With the ever-quickening pace of the budding years of the 21st century, society might be self-diagnosed as having Attention Deficit Disorder. Often people do not sup or dine at home or restaurants; they choose any one of thousands of fast food *outlets*. Many people gain knowledge of current events via media sound-bytes and/or

---

[d] an earlier work by this author.

photo-ops. People seem unable to dedicate the time or inclination to read classic literature. People elect to subject themselves to the proliferation of violence in cinema, song lyrics and television. Violence provides a sort of "crack hit" of shock and/or titillation. American broadcast media is incapable of providing one twenty-four period of violence-free *programming*. In this case the double-entendre is intended and appropriate. Media is a victim of its own programming when, in the case of the 32 murders at Virginia Tech they, most predictably and most regrettably, could not refrain from providing national "coverage" (to include photos and rants) of a multiple assassin and in so doing, blessing him with notoriety. But then why should the attention given to a deranged man be any different from the deranged religi-bomber who practices the same terrorist behavior and becomes media-martyred. What might this indicate about a society that seemingly thirsts for a steady media diet of vicarious crime, murder, rape, or physical and emotional aggression? Some people breed certain types of dogs to be violent. Do we not inbreed violence within our own society? Has violence become a type of emotional morphine, and if so, to deaden what pain?

The mid-to-late 19th century gave rise to several schools of painting. In America the Hudson River School came to prominence when artists such as Church, Cole, Kensett, Durand, and Bierstadt interpreted the natural world and rendered landscapes infused with beauty and an optimism that was characteristic to American life after the Civil War. Russia produced the "Wanderers" or "Nomads". Kramskoy, Repin, Ge, Volkov, etc, lent a virtuosity and poignancy to the hardships and suffering of peasant life in Czarist Russia. Names of the great Impressionists of France are well known, Renoir, Degas,

Monet, Cezanne, etc. Though, perhaps not as readily familiar as the French, are the names of American Impressionists such as Tarbell, Hassam, Chase, Reid, Benson, etc. These Americans along with Remington and Russell, artists of the American West, effectively brought optimism, a joie-de-vivre to their art that brought inspiration to a wide range of people who had artistic inclinations.

The 20th century saw the passing of these formal schools of artistic expression only to give way to, for lack of a better, or more formally recognized term, art of deconstructionist expression. From Gustav Klimt and Edvard Munch (who painted *Despair*, later called *The Scream*), to Dada, cubism, and hence, abstract impressionism, this deconstructionism may have been the emotional prelude to political upheavals in the offing.

Beginning again with the latter part of the 19th century a transformation occurs in classical music. The classicism of Tchaikovsky and Rachmaninoff is challenged at the beginning of the early twentieth century by the Second Viennese School atonal conjurations of Alban Berg and Arnold Schoenberg. In the 21st century we are able to enjoy the musical genius of such people as John Williams and James Newton Howard, but rare is the talent and the manner of expression of such men.

Architecturally we have abandoned the character of stone and iron of the great European capitals, forsaking them for skyscrapers of glass and steel. These towering structures state a case for economically plausible expressions of technology and function however these buildings lack the soul and gravitas of the cities of our western heritage. Small European towns, often have a church at the city center. In small town America, quite often, a courthouse stands in the town square in lieu of a house of worship. Conceivably the case can be made that in conforming to economic law and juris law, we have failed to focus on, and thus have suffered the consequences of, the waning of beauty and morality from day-to-day life. Beauty and morality have become as abstract as modern art. Life imitates art and art imitates life.

If one assumes that the art of mankind represents the condition of mankind, one can see that the deconstructionist influence in the arts and the proliferation of violence in broadcast media has apparently become a type of morphine that assuages spiritual pain. Were religion-based faith more fulfilling, the seeming need for emotional morphine (sex, drugs, violence) would not be as compelling and perhaps art would be focused on expressions of beauty not the abstract or vulgar.

Realization of faith in self, faith in our fellow man, faith in the Great Integrity, faith in Goodness is an oasis of true spiritual expression. We must begin to redirect our focus from ecto-religion to endo-spirituality. Focus should be centered on the value of reconstituting our reservoirs of creative beauty and devoting ourselves to the pursuit of emotional wellness and spiritual wholeness, rather than upon the immediacy of a quick fix of violence and hate. When Michelangelo sculpted the Vatican's Pieta, it was not the beauty of the Pieta that was on display but the beauty of expression of the soul of Michelangelo himself. Quoting Michelangelo (1475-1564), "A man paints with his brains not with his hands." Four centuries later French writer Emile Zola (1840-1902) was of similar mind, "There are two men inside the artist, the poet and the craftsman. One is born a poet. One becomes a craftsman." Art is the expression of spirit emulating the

Divinity from which it arose. Indeed Michelangelo, "The true work of art is but a shadow of the divine perfection."

Birds and bees, flora and fauna, have awareness yet they are unable to pursue and acquire knowledge. King Louis XVI of France, in the late 18th century spoke of the power of knowledge. "Louis XVI, seeing in his Temple prison the works of Voltaire and Rousseau said, "Those two men have destroyed France," – meaning his dynasty. "The Bourbons might have preserved themselves," said Napoleon, "if they had controlled writing materials. The advent of cannon killed the feudal system; ink will kill the modern social organization." "Books rule the world," said Voltaire, "or at least those nations in it which have a written language; the others do not count." "Nothing enfranchises like education"; - and he proceeded to enfranchise France. "When once a nation begins to think, it is impossible to stop it."[10]

Just as Gandhi said "Poverty is the worst form of violence", so ignorance is the worst form of bondage. When referring to the oppressive poverty of his homeland (India) Gandhi was, evidently, speaking of bodily poverty, that of finance, material, and basic sustenance. In this context he was absolutely correct. Regarding poverty as defined in the United States, the Department Of Health and Human Services has established a poverty line whereby annually, any single person (Hawaii and Alaska notwithstanding) earning less than $9800 or any couple earning $13,200, is considered poor, in a state of poverty. For sake of circumstance however, let us assume Gandhi was speaking of spiritual poverty. Were that the case, Gandhi's observation would have been no less profound. It would be difficult indeed to determine a "spiritual poverty line". If however, a spiritual poverty line were stipulated such that someone would be considered spiritually poor if a) they want to be someone else, b) want a life circumstance other than what it is, or c) look past today seeking fulfillment, more people would be considered in spiritual poverty than material poverty.

One cause of spiritual poverty is the prohibition of spiritual thought considered unorthodox, or worse, heretic. "Heresy" derives its original definition from roots in the Late Latin "haeresis", or Late Greek "hairesis", which meant merely "to choose". The Merriam-Webster Dictionary currently states the definition of heresy as "adherence to a religious opinion contrary to church dogma". Heresy has come to mean "choose wrongly" thus suffering ostracism and punishment. Church founding father Tertullian wanted to limit verbal dissent. "But Tertullian insists that making choices is evil, since choice destroys group unity. To stamp out heresy, Tertullian says, church leaders must not allow people to ask questions, for it is "questions that make people heretics"…."The true Christian, Tertullian declares, simply determines to "know nothing…at variance with the truth of faith." But when people "insist on asking about the issues that concern them,". Tertullian says, "We have a moral obligation to refute them…. They say that we must ask questions in order to discuss," Tertullian continues, "but what is there to discuss?" When the "heretics" object that Christians must discuss what the Scriptures really mean, Tertullian declares that believers must dismiss all argument over scriptural interpretation; such controversy only "has the effect of upsetting the stomach or the brain."[11] Quoting Thomas Carlyle again, "I don't like to talk much with people who always agree with me. It is amusing to coquette with an echo for a little while, but one soon tires of it." Robert A. Heinlein was more blunt, "I never learned from a man who agreed with me." And not to put to fine a point on the matter, quoting American novelist Nathaniel Hawthorne (1804-

1864), "It contributes greatly towards a man's moral and intellectual health, to be brought into habits of companionship with individuals unlike himself, who care little for his pursuits, and whose sphere and abilities he must go out of himself to appreciate."

Further, houses of worship, be they churches, synagogues, temples, or mosques, are branch offices of the religion they represent, i.e. spiritual franchises. The preacher, pastor, priest, rabbi, imam, mullah, are but franchisees who present orthodox faith as they understand it to be with little if any tolerance for heterodox positions and certainly no tolerance whatsoever for positions deemed heretical. In the world of commerce, no less an entrepreneur than Ray Kroc (founder of McDonald's Corp.) emulated Tertullian and his colleagues in similar manner. One can only imagine how Tertullian perceived his role as a theologian when considering how Ray Kroc explained his mission, "I didn't invent the hamburger. I just took it more seriously than anyone else." Having done so, Mr. Kroc also commented, "We will not tolerate nonconformists." When Tertullian won his tug-of-war with Pelagius and those of the Pelagian school of thought who advocated for the essential goodness of man, Tertullian had all of them excommunicated and deemed heretics. Tertullian's soul mate, Ray Kroc, "Competition? Send 'em south, if they're gonna drown put a hose in their mouth."

Religious thought-police have warped the definition of heresy into thought-crime. "Clearly the person who accepts the church as an infallible guide will believe whatever the church teaches" – Thomas Aquinas (1225-1274). Free will is maximized when exposed to opportunities afforded by knowledge, thought, and theory. Free will is minimized when intimidated by constricts of dogma and doctrine. Ecclesiastical ostracism began in the second century after Christ when Irenaeus selected gospels for canonization and continued through the fourth century when Tertullian authored original sin into the "party line". Ostracization continues to the present day with condemnation of Father Pierre Tielhard de Chardin (1881-1955). Tielhard de Chardin would have been differently disposed to Tertullian's "true Christian" as evidenced by his belief in Noosphere and Omega Point. But the power of his faith is undeniable as evidenced by this quote, "Someday, after mastering the winds, the waves, the tides and gravity, we shall harness for God the energies of love, and then, for a second time in the history of the world, man will have discovered fire."

The church finds the spiritual fire of Tielhard de Chardin intimidating because of the veracity of his belief and his courage to state it. Religious dogma is the equivalent of a spiritual prophylactic. The hindering of spiritual expression or spiritual curiosity should have no bounds as each person has the self-evident right to pursue their own beliefs to their own destiny; not someone else's thought toward someone else's idea of what their destiny should be. Each person is a statement of divinity not to be herded into a flock but to soar as an eagle on the thought-wings of freedom of choice. Each human being has the divine right, the divine independence to seek answers to his own questions in his own way.

Each of Homo Divinitas represents the sum of consequence of choices relating to his or her existence within the realm of duality. Virtually any event or action contains a minimum of two outcomes that hinge on the fulcrum of decision. The balance of decision will tilt toward "I want" or "I do not want". The outcome of any particular choice is the sum of interplay between knowledge, discipline, and ethical value on one hand and ignorance, apathy, or sloth on the other. Physical law states that "things in motion tend to stay in motion, things at rest tend to stay at rest." Those who want to be active and remain inactive have a greater want to be sedentary. Those who want to lose weight and do not have a greater want not to make the effort to lose weight.

The question is posed, "How old would you be if you didn't know your birthday?" Further, how would you know your weight without a scale? Fitness of body and mind are nuclei of the same atom of being. Fitness should not be measured by clock or scale, but rather by the sovereign act of self-determination. Physical or emotional metabolism notwithstanding, the application of principles, ethics and morals; and the discipline of method and manner of choice effect the ethereal as surely as the corporeal. This author recently chose to engage in a fat-loss regimen. I also chose not to weigh myself or determine a target weight. Weight loss occurred however the primary intention was to apply a regimen of discipline to physical body just as I apply intellectual and emotional discipline to the mind. In 1992 while living in Pago Pago, AmericanSamoa, I suffered a severe cerebral concussion during Hurricane Val resulting in loss of the senses of taste and smell. Nevertheless, my fat-loss experience reinforced the view that eating food is primarily habitual. What becomes manifest in life is regarding the equations and subsequent results of wants and choices with enough determination to influence the fulcrum of decision toward long-term benefit. A self-fulfilling future consists of self-fulfilled nows strung together. The force of discipline and/or determination must exceed force of habit or the inertia of sloth.

Regarding choice and result, each human being (Homo Divinitas) also has the *responsibility* and onus to exercise courage to those ends.

Homo Divinitas also bears responsibility should he choose *not* to exercise courage to seek physical and/or spiritual fulfillment. Each human being is a self-contained soul residing in a cathedral of body. Each of us represents the sum of our choices and are subject to, and responsible for, our destiny and the course thereto. Spiritus mundi, such as it is, necessarily needs a greater effort to reverse course than maintain one. Often, desire may wish to change course however strength and discipline must supplement desire to support and maintain change. Quoting a tongue–in–cheek comment by author Erica Jong (*Fear of Flying*), "Take your life into your own hands and what happens? A terrible thing: no one to blame." What was left unsaid is that wonderful things happen too, pride of self-expression, dignity in bearing responsibility, and self-realization through the freedom and artistry of creating and fulfilling one's own destiny. "A man's character is his destiny." – Heroclytus.

INVICTUS by William Ernest Henley (1849 – 1903)

Out of the night that covers me,
  Black as the Pit from pole to pole,
I thank whatever gods may be
  For my unconquerable soul.

In the fell clutch of circumstance   5
  I have not winced nor cried aloud.
Under the bludgeonings of chance
  My head is bloody, but unbowed.

Beyond this place of wrath and tears
  Looms but the Horror of the shade,   10
And yet the menace of the years

Finds, and shall find, me unafraid.

It matters not how strait the gate,
 How charged with punishments the scroll,
I am the master of my fate: *15*
 I am the captain of my soul.

Homo Divinitas is indeed master and captain on the voyage to destiny's shore. Quoting Michelangelo, "The greater danger for most of us lies not in setting our aim too high and falling short; but in setting our aim too low, and achieving our mark." Homo Divinitas has unlimited potential yet we have the tendency to disdain possibility in lieu of the practical or the predictable.

When Beethoven referred to the creative impulse as consulting with a Goddess, he did so with the same ardor as Nietzsche. One is reminded again of the sublime thought of Khalil Gibran, "One seeks me in prayer and the other in pain. And in the spirit of each there is a bower for my spirit."[12]

The Gideon Society used to donate bibles to hotels so believers would not be without scripture. On a recent visit to India my wife and I stayed at the Oberoi Amarvilas. The hotel provided not a bible but a book entitled *I Am My Best Self* by Dipa De Motwane. The author did not copyright the work yet all proceeds go to charity.[e] Quoting from *I Am My Best Self*, "You were born to create. Whether planting a garden, cooking a meal, writing a letter, building a friendship or painting a picture, your Best Self wants to

---

[e] My compliments to Dipa De Motwane and the Amarvilas on their collaborative efforts.

be expressed through you. We all have talent. Each of us has been given something special to offer the world. It doesn't matter if it's big or small, whether you are a genius or not, the act of creation brings out the best in you." The Gideon Society donated bibles intending to serve a pre-existing audience or to proselytize. *I Am My Best Self* offers universal wisdom and veracity.

CHAPTER 5
EMOTIONAL WHOLENESS

"If thou wilt make a man happy, add not unto his riches but take away from his desires."
– Epicurus (341BC – 271BC).

"I never submitted the whole system of my opinions to the creed of any party of men whatever, in religion, in philosophy, in politics or in anything else, where I was capable of thinking for myself. Such an addiction is the last degradation of a free and moral agent. If I could not go to heaven but with a party, I would not go there at all."
– Thomas Jefferson.

"If they answer not to thy call walk alone,
If they are afraid and cower mutely facing the wall,
O thou of evil luck,
Open thy mind and speak out alone.
If they turn away, and desert you when crossing the wilderness,
O thou of evil luck,
Trample the thorns under thy tread, and along the blood-lined track travel alone.
If they do not hold up the light when the night is troubled with storm,
O thou of evil luck,
With the thunder flame of pain ignite thy own heart and let it burn alone."
– Bengali poet Rabindranath Tagore (1861-1941).

More than flora and fauna, Homo Divinitas is uniquely capable of *faith*. Faith is an intellectual/emotional non-rational exercise that acknowledges the existence of the unproved and un-provable. More than flora and fauna, Homo Divinitas is uniquely capable of *hope.* Still further, Homo Divinitas is capable of *charity*, i.e an act or feeling of generosity. Each of these traits is found only in the domain of humanity. These attributes are not to be found in the animal kingdom.

When Charles Darwin attempted to place Homo sapiens within the domain of the ape, he failed however, to address the supra-natural human behavior that runs *contrary* to his thesis. The locus of such behavior includes yet is not limited to, faith, hope and charity. Homo Divinitas possesses an extraordinary capacity for empathy, charity, forgiveness, and love. Examples exist within the animal kingdom of affection and parental care, however occasionally human beings possess and demonstrate these traits to others more than themselves and occasionally with cost to self. The act of charity is contrary to survival of the fittest. To the extent mankind can relish in these unique actions, to the extent mankind can implement these divine gifts which are truly his own, he can direct a world more in keeping with a divine context of being.

Emotional and spiritual wholeness is a journey worth the effort no matter the destination. Remembering Michelangelo's quote, to the extent a person reaches for the stars, one becomes better for having reached. English poet and playwright Robert Browning (1812-1889) was of like mind, "Ah, but a man's reach should exceed his grasp, or what's a heaven for?" Reaching the star is not as significant as the effort put forth in reaching for the star. Failure happens only when one fails to try. Success is not the opposite of failure; accomplishment is the opposite of failure. Success is relative to effort put forth in attempting to achieve accomplishment and may manifest in unintended ways. Failure is primarily a temporary interpretation of words or actions, which may or may not change during the course of time. Still, success is determined by the non-acceptance of failure. One of the elements of spirituality, which may have debilitating ramifications, is misconstruing the concept of duality when regarding terms such as good or bad, right or wrong, negative or positive. In most instances when considering the concepts of "right and wrong" a more precise terminology may be terms such as, accurate or inaccurate, valid or invalid, correct or incorrect, factual or erroneous. Surely, adjectives may be used as yardsticks to describe polarities and areas in-between. One may also remember that each polarity of existence defines the other, indeed could not exist without the other.

The Great Integrity created a perfect universe, "perfect" in this sense being defined as "in unison with karma and Truth", as opposed to perfection being defined as "action or object without error or flaw." Understanding that "perfect" or "flawed" represents man's subjective evaluation of any given word or deed, qua any other, at any given moment. Chaos results when mankind's perception of the universe and behavior in it, is subject to the maelstrom of conflicting judgments, interpretations, justifications, and meanings that mankind assigns to and heaps upon any particular endeavor, all of which are subject to perception, change, or reinterpretation. Flaws do exist however they do so only in man's perception of, and experience with his own actions amidst the divine creation of Divinity. Philosophy or theology may wish to consider that Creation is perfection and that mankind must accept the responsibility and ramifications of his and her own actions. One cannot presume to understand the inertia that drives human events however please keep in mind a beautiful Zen paradigm, "The snow falls, each flake in its appropriate place." One can presume to understand that we, and the ethos we create, are subject to the destiny we choose to realize.

The concept of the Great Integrity, God, Allah exists. On this, all people of faith will agree. On what they may not agree is the persona of the Creator. Muslims consider it blasphemous to portray an image of Allah. Christianity portrays God as a male of Caucasian race such as the rendering of the ceiling of the Cistine Chapel of Saint Paul in the Vatican. It may be interesting to consider the following thought by a Professor of Theology from Maynooth College, Ireland. I quote Dr. Miceal Ledwith from the compelling movie, *What the Bleep Do We Know*, "But I am at one with the Great Being that made me and brought me here and that formed the galaxies and universes et cetera. How did that get taken out of religion? It was not hard. Most of the problems that religion and various philosophical movements down through the centuries have produced have been errors because that's where they started. That God is a separate being from us, to whom I must offer worship; whom I must cultivate, humor, please, and hope to obtain a reward from, at the very end of my life. That is not what God is. That is a blasphemy."[13]

Further, it may be interesting to consider that God/Allah/the Great Integrity may not have a face at all, never mind that it should be that of John Carter (nee Charleton Heston). I saw the face of God when I was in a monastery in the town of Gyantse in western Tibet. Divinity, the face of God, came to me *in the form of* two abandoned, starving, dying young puppies. As we were leaving the Monastery I noticed a tiny puppy (perhaps not yet one month old) that apparently had been discarded and left to die in the bowels of a public latrine. When I went over to tend to the puppy, I could hear the whimpering of another puppy near a little window in a little nook under the latrine. Our Tibetan guide Lha Lha, was able, in spite of considerable stench, to reach the second puppy and bring him through the window into the courtyard with his little brother. Their pathetic fragile young bodies were covered in feces. I initiated efforts to water, feed, bathe, and comfort the two puppies. Someone then brought a large cardboard box that I lined with my jacket so they would have comfort and warmth. On this part of my journey, I was accompanied by an airport-administrator cum veterinary assistant who told me (once the episode was over) that the puppies were within hours of death. Quite soon thereafter she, her husband, and several others helped tend to these beautiful puppies. They also lent me a jacket so I could be warm. I started crying with exquisite joy when each puppy started to raise their tails and come to life and summon enough energy to lick my face and hands with their tiny little tongues in response the *first kindness* they had ever known. I knew as I hugged and cradled those loving puppies that my Creator had hugged and cradled my soul.

Deity visits us every day in forms we do not recognize. Deity confronts us in cognito whenever a living being approaches in genuine need of kindness, understanding, tenderness, and love. The fullness of soul experienced and rendered through the act of giving to persons or puppies is the caress of Divinity. I had always lived my life from a point of empathy and the Golden Rule, *yet on this occasion, with a death consequence in the offing, I **understood** what this is all about.* Having been through that epiphany, I recognize Divinity everywhere. Duality is the domain in which, we have the exquisite option to render kindness and understanding or selfishness and callousness, honor or dishonor to ourselves, others, and all who share the magnificence of Creation.

Duality can be confusing when stated both in terms of the here-and-now and the afterlife. Quoting verse LXVI from The Rubaiyat, by Omar Khayyam:

I sent my soul through the Invisible,
Some letter of that After-life to spell:
And by and by my Soul retunr'd to me,
And answer'd "I Myself am Heav'n and Hell.

Further, "The mind is its own place, and in itself, can make Heaven of hell, and a hell of Heaven." – John Milton (1608-1674).

Taking Milton's quote to heart, one might suggest that the spiritus mundi of Homo Divinitas under the aegis of religious thought as contained in the bible and Qu'ran have created the hell on earth preached for evil-doers upon "death". Mankind is the enabler of his own destiny. Our actions create the environment in which we live and we are consigned by the immutable laws of karma to enjoy or suffer the wholeness of moral behavior or the lack thereof. When, by our own actions, we vow and subsequently commit to helping our fellow man, woman, and child, the other men, women, and children taking that same vow are simultaneously committing to help us. World peace and tranquility will become so, only when each of us have the moral certitude to acknowledge that it is better to give than to receive, that honor is better than dishonor, that with forgiveness and atonement, the burden of our own faults is relieved.

Homo Divinitas must, indeed must, redefine the meaning and ramification of what constitutes wholesome behavior and then have the courage to realize that behavior. Behavior and activities are deemed beneficial if, and only if, the consequences of those actions provide or cause mutual wellness for the parties involved. This is not to say that doing good deeds for someone else is done so in anticipation of reciprocity, it should not. Action that benefits another person is alone, sufficient of its own action. In other words, a good deed *is* its own reward. Further, if, after you tell someone you love him or her, you expect something in return, you have missed the point of the exercise. Love is a joy to express and mutual love is a many splendored thing yet the essential point is to feel the emotion of love and just be with the wholeness that love bequeaths without asking for anything in return.

"Progress" such as it is currently understood, has brought mankind to the brink of space and technology has made life easier yet how much progress have we made in realizing and experiencing love and happiness, and towards what are we progressing? Progress merely means forward direction, which is meaningless if the direction in which we are headed is the wrong one. Quoting Doctor Rollo May, "…that the chief problem of people in the middle decade of the twentieth century is *emptiness*. By that I mean not only that many people do not know what they want; they often do not have any clear idea of what they feel. When they talk about lack of autonomy, or lament their ability to make decisions - difficulties which are present in all decades – it soon becomes evident that their underlying problem is that they have no definite experience of their own desires or wants. Thus they feel swayed this way and that, with painful feelings of powerlessness, because they feel vacuous, empty. The complaint which leads them to me for help may be, for example, that their love relationships always break up or that they cannot go through with marriage plans or are dissatisfied with the marriage partner. But they do not talk long before they make it clear that they expect the marriage partner, real or hoped for, to fill some lack, some vacancy within themselves; and they are anxious and angry because he or she doesn't."[14]

Continuing Dr. May's quote, "They generally talk fluently about what they *should* want – to complete their college degrees successfully, to get a job, to fall in love and marry and raise a family – but it is soon evident, even to them, that they are describing what others, parents, professors, employers, expect of them rather than what they themselves want."[15] This author wishes to add, "or have". Wealth and/or possessions have nothing to do with happiness or spiritual fulfillment.

People who are empty or unhappy complain and blame other people for their own unhappiness, i.e. "you make me so mad!" or "you don't make me happy". Unhappiness may also manifest through self-inhibition, "I won't be happy unless…" Certainly a person who makes such a precondition precluding happiness will *not* be happy until (if ever) the condition is met. Statements such as this are an open-ended sentence to unhappiness and are probably not stand-alone statements. If someone has a penchant for such "roadblock reasoning", if one roadblock is negotiated, another self-imposed roadblock is likely to follow. Happiness is a choice. Happy people choose a way to be happy and unhappy people choose a way to be unhappy, that is why each is so.

On a personal level, emptiness can result from relying on another person to fill our own needs. However, on a societal level, the same vacuum exists because organized religion has, quite evidently, been unable to quench mankind's spiritual thirst. The emptiness to which Dr. May refers when describing his patients at the micro personal level bespeaks samodaya on the macro societal level. To a great extent, other persons and other institutions of missionary religious doctrine have not been able to fulfill the spiritual upreach of mankind because, ipso facto, the world seeks and pursues amoral answers and/or unwholesome cures to anesthetize the pain of emptiness and samodaya. If organized religion had provided adequate answers to man's pursuit of spirituality throughout the centuries, spiritus mundi would not be awash in an overwhelming torrent of spiritual morphine evident in material consumption, sexual promiscuity, violence, and terrorism.

Statements such as "this or that will make me happy" are fallacious in the sense that whatever this or that may be, one can be happy *without* whatever it may be. Statements from the Qu'ran, Old Testament, and New Testament, fraught with violence, and the emotional manipulation of conditional love are contrary to finding answers for spiritual liberty, fraternity, and egality. The wisdom of songwriter, singer, and entertainer Kenny Rogers ranks with the great philosophers when he speaks of gamblers and poker players, " 'cause every hand's a winner and every hand's a loser". Whether gambler or philosopher, prince or beggar, the rules are the same. All hands are determined by what are made of them. A wise woman unrelated to Mr. Rogers once commented, play the cards you get better, and you'll get better cards.

Each person (Homo Divinitas) bears the responsibility of determining and experiencing happiness and fulfillment as they so determine them to be. Unhappiness is caused in direct proportion to the extent one cedes emotional sovereignty to the control of someone else. This is not to say that happiness cannot be shared. To the contrary, happiness is best when shared...bearing in mind that the truest happiness is born of independence not dependence.

These points may seem contrary to religious thought and in some quarters they are. To quote from *A New Reformation*, "Many if not all formal organized religions present a carrot to a mule, a reward (heaven) for beliefs and/or actions consistent with established scripture.[16] Regarding our outward physical appearance in heaven, it is theorized that we will look as our most beautiful selves. The unspoken assumption being that no one will have acne, or be overweight, or have a physical deformity. Authors of gospel text of any religion do the afterlife a disservice when the best they can do is portray heaven by pandering to vanity (outward beauty), greed (all manner of precious stones and gold), and sexual gratification (promiscuity). Rather than describing heaven, such "revelations" regarding the nature of the setting in which afterlife occurs bear a more striking resemblance to the pleasure-palace of Xanadu in the poem *Kubla Khan* by the English poet and philosopher Samuel Taylor Coleridge (1772-1834). This hollow religious equivalent of "bait and switch" represents the shallowness of desires of the flesh fulfilled, not the epitome of self-esteem and spiritual transcendence of morals and ethics over material temptation. The blasphemers who write of the outward beauty of the people who populate heaven failed to consider that beauty has nothing to do with the shape or feature of someone's face or body. True beauty is expressed with affection of the heart, the caress of a hug, truth and integrity in word, action, and thought.

"For those who freely choose any particular path of worship, may those blessings arise in abundance. That being the case though, one could question the existential motive of the individual. How

"Christian" would someone be if not for Christ? With the gospels as a compass, a good deed is only a commodity bartered for salvation. Is the believer only doing good deeds under the threat of eternal damnation? If so, does this not demean the deed itself as it is done under emotional extortion and threat of spiritual damnation?"[17]

The emotional wellness of wholesome behavior is a natural stepladder to abundant self-esteem. Self-esteem establishes a personal freedom of not being dependent on the whim or esteem of other people. Insecurities of others may be directed in the form of unwarranted verbal assaults and/or masking envy by withholding genuine praise. An invisible insult may take the form of a compliment not expressed. The world has already seen too much hurt. Abundance of self-esteem indemnifies the strong of spirit against the insecurities of the weak who do not have the courage to admit weakness and thus will always remain weak. Abundance of self-esteem indemnifies against misdirected affection. The 17th century French writer Francois de la Rochefoucauld, "Jealousy springs more from love of self than the love of another." When speaking of flattery, Monsieur Rochefoucauld was as perceptive when he opined, "Flattery is a kind of bad money to which our vanity gives us currency." Name-calling (sticks-and-stones) is a reflection of the weakness of the person who demeans another person. Diatribes, bigotry, flattery, hate, jealousy are an autobiography of the speaker, not the listener.

Anger, when expressed in any arena, is an expression of self. Reasons are used to "justify" anger. "Just" or not, anger consumes only those who are angry. Understanding, tolerance, and self-esteem can in large measure, eliminate anger. Some people become angry in a traffic jam, others do not. Some people choose to harbor anger others do not. Quoting Frederick Langbridge (1849-1923), "Two men look out from the same bars; one sees the mud, and one the stars." Anger and hate are reflections of self, manifested toward others. Some people choose to be happy other people choose unhappiness. The phrase, "He makes me so angry", is a phrase we have all heard. Though, if the statement is accurately dissected, what is really happening is, "I willingly cede my peace of mind in order to participate in someone else's anger." Nobody can make you angry without your permission. "Holding on to anger is like grasping a hot coal with the intent of throwing it at someone else; you are the one who gets burned." – Buddha. Some people possess a hate so pervasive and compelling they blow up themselves and others while many people possessing love are missionaries of understanding and toleration.

"Unhappiness or negativity is a disease on our planet. What pollution is on the outer level is negativity on the inner. It is everywhere, not just in the places where people don't have enough, but even more so where they have more than enough. Is that surprising? No. The affluent world is even more deeply identified with form, more lost in content, more trapped in ego. People believe themselves to be dependent on what happens for their happiness, that is to say, dependent on form. They don't realize that what happens is the most unstable thing in the universe. It changes constantly. They look upon the present moment as either marred by something that has happened and shouldn't have or as deficient because of something that has not happened but should have."[18]

The following seemingly anonymous work is entitled *My Life*.

My life is but a weaving
Between the Lord and me.
I may not choose the colors,

He knows what they should be;
For He can view the pattern
Upon the upper side.
Sometimes He weaveth sorrow,
Which seems strange to me;
But I will trust His judgement
And work on faithfully.
Tis He who fills the shuttle,
And He who knows what is best,
So I shall weave in earnest
Leaving to Him the rest.
Not till the loom is silent
And the shuttles cease to fly
Shall God unroll the canvas
And explain the reason why
The dark threads are as needed
In the Weaver's skillful hand
As the threads of gold and silver
In the pattern He has planned.

A large part of emotional and spiritual wellness is the acceptance of the *entire* creation of the Great Integrity not just those "rewards" from God that appeal to ego. Egos emulate God when we think we know what is best for our lives. However, is it not profoundly pretentious to second-guess the magnificence of creation? Quoting the Swiss psychiatrist Carl Jung (1875 – 1961), "Even a happy life cannot be without a measure of darkness, and the word happy would lose it's meaning if it were not balanced by sadness. It is far better to take things as they come along with patience and equanimity." When a parent takes a child to a physician for an immunization, the child feels pain and recoils against the pain of the needle. Upon the advent of further immunizations our parents tell us, contrary to our every instinct, the pain must be suffered for good reason. With faith in the word of our parents, contrary to our instincts, we submit to the pain of the inoculation. Yet, on a grander scale, as adults our petulant egos are so fully fledged as to assume adversity is a punishment or inconvenience thrust upon us and have the audacity to ask God not to do it "His" way, or second-guess why He should not do it *our* way. Our temerity compels us to seek the way of least resistance, to deny the crucible of adversity though the Physician has prescribed such medicine as immunizations against further more substantial pain.

Complaint is the manifestation of guilt of making "wrong" choices. People complain when someone else betrays a secret they could not themselves keep. Complaint is easier than bearing the burden of responsibility. Incidentally, success more often than not is betrothed to persons of diligence and/or patience. If one accepts that decisions were best made under the circumstances, there is no resultant guilt. Guilt need not exist if one considers that in any situation, if one does his or her best, matters will result, as they should, *regardless* of outcome. It matters not if one wins or loses, it does matter that one does ones best. In fact, to the extent we externalize the creation of which we are a part (leave it to God, put it in His hands) to that same extent, we cause our own condition by failing to improve it. The phrase "God helps those who help themselves" may be a prima facie acknowledgement that we are divine. Quoting a lyric from a song from the 1970's rock group America, "Oz never did give nothin' to the Tin Man that he didn't already have." This is not to say that we have all we need, far from it. Nevertheless, we certainly have the wherewithal to treat our fellow man with the same courtesy we ourselves desire or expect. All of us have heard the mini-prayer "God bless you". That's all well and good but we have the ability here and now to bless each other with kindness, tenderness, and mercy. The infinite nature of the Great Integrity may never be defined with finite terms yet one matter is certain, nothing can be lost if we start treating each other as elements of the divine. Perhaps then, the power of love will overcome the love of power and Homo Divinitas will thrive amid brotherhood.

Freedom is an essential component of mental, emotional, and spiritual right-mindedness. Freedom can be measured in many ways... freedom of speech, freedom of movement, there is also freedom from emotional predators who wish to restrict speech, thought, and movement by preying on those who are not strong of will or spirit. Freedom is independence, and conversely, dependence is the antithesis of freedom. Dependence is a type of slavery and slavery has many masters. Slavery is dependence. Addiction is dependence. Persons willingly or unwillingly cede freedom (independence) in direct proportion to the extent he or she participates in various forms of dependency. Dependency may be viewed traditionally as habitual use of drugs (legal or illegal), alcohol, or nicotine. A more subtle form of dependence is the subjugation of emotional wellness to the concept of victimization. Victimization can be benign such as, "you have offended me", or more sinister, "my ancestors were slaves". This is not to minimize or condone American Apartheid or deny that emotional offenses occur in any theater of human endeavor, yet the fact of the matter is that nobody can anticipate the emotional thresholds of another person. This is not to minimize pain and/or suffering in any circumstance, nevertheless, quoting the venerable Chinese philosopher Confucius, "To be wronged is nothing unless you choose to remember it." A case can be made that it is immoral for succeeding generations of African-Americans to ask for compensation for the slavery of their ancestors by piggy-backing on the strong shoulders of their forebears who bore genuine pain, sorrow, and suffering more often than not with a dignity lacking in those who seek vicarious compensation. The tragic immorality of the circumstance is that innocent persons have assumed the mantle of victimization and choose to emulate the victims they champion in search of something for nothing.

Persons may act in a boorish or offensive manner or act in immoral ways however, please consider that behavior is a reflection of the person behaving badly, not of those to whom the behavior is directed. The individual, who may elect to subjugate his or her emotional wellbeing to the behavior of a lout, willingly submits to victimization. Someone weak of spirit may latch onto someone else's rude behavior and be "hooked" into an antagonistic confrontation in order to "set him straight". The immature ego will seek and feel "justification" in "putting someone in their place" when in fact, the boor had already done a perfect job of that all by himself. One never wins an argument with a fool so it's even more foolish to argue with one. Apology and atonement notwithstanding, Karmic Law will determine appropriate consequence for all behavior. The spiritually sovereign individual has the capability to choose peace over conflict. The spiritually sovereign individual has the wisdom to set the example for those who follow.

Setting the example will provide segue of sorts. Consider as an example, the Old Testament account of the rendering by Moses of Ten Commandments given to him by God. Setting the scene (with comments and questions in parenthesis) as told in King James Version of Exodus 19:10-25:

[10] And the LORD said unto Moses, Go unto the people, and sanctify them today and tomorrow, and let them wash their clothes,

[11] And be ready against the third day: for the third day the LORD will come down in the sight of all the people upon mount Sinai.

[12] And thou shalt set bounds unto the people round about, saying, Take heed to yourselves, that ye go not up into the mount, or touch the border of it: whosoever toucheth the mount shall be surely put to death. (Why would God execute those eager to hear His word? Doesn't execution seem somewhat harsh?)

[13] There shall not a hand touch it, but he shall surely be stoned, or shot through; whether it be beast or man, it shall not live: when the trumpet soundeth long, they shall come up to the mount.

[14] And Moses went down from the mount unto the people, and sanctified the people; and they washed their clothes.

[15] And he said unto the people, "Be ready against the third day: come not at your wives. (Come not at your wives is translated by the NIV as "abstain from sexual relations." So to heighten the drama and suspense, a three-day delay, clean clothes and, of course, no sex.)

[16] And it came to pass on the third day in the morning, that there were thunders and lightnings, and a thick cloud upon the mount, and the voice of the trumpet exceeding loud; so that all the people that was in the camp trembled. (Melodrama and abject *fear*)

[17] And Moses brought forth the people out of the camp to meet with God; and they stood at the nether part of the mount.

[18] And mount Sinai was altogether on a smoke, because the LORD descended upon it in fire: and the smoke thereof ascended as the smoke of a furnace, and the whole mount quaked greatly. (Of course, more melodrama, more fear. Fire and smoke emanate from burning objects. What airborne combustible objects burned causing fire and smoke? Would not a sunny day have been more appropriate for "His" Commandments?)

[19] And when the voice of the trumpet sounded long, and waxed louder and louder, Moses spake, and God answered him by a voice. (How large was that trumpet? More melodrama.)

[20] And the LORD came down upon mount Sinai, on the top of the mount: and the LORD called Moses up to the top of the mount; and Moses went up. (How long did God have to wait for Moses to scale 7498-foot Mount Sinai?)

[21] And the LORD said unto Moses, Go down, charge the people, lest they break through unto the LORD to gaze, and many of them perish.

[22] And let the priests also, which come near to the LORD, sanctify themselves, lest the LORD break forth upon them.

[23] And Moses said unto the LORD, The people cannot come up to mount Sinai: for thou chargedst us, saying, Set bounds about the mount, and sanctify it. (HAD PERFECT GOD FORGOTTEN?)

[24] And the LORD said unto him, Away, get thee down, and thou shalt come up, thou, and Aaron with thee: but let not the priests and the people break through to come up unto the LORD, lest he break forth upon them.

[25] So Moses went down unto the people, and spake unto them.

At this point Moses descends Mount Sinai and speaks the following excerpted words as related in Exodus 20:

[3] Thou shalt have no other gods before me.

[4] Thou shalt not make unto thee any graven image, or any likeness of any thing that is in heaven above, or that is in the earth beneath, or that is in the water under the earth.

[7] Thou shalt not take the name of the LORD thy God in vain; for the LORD will not hold him guiltless that taketh his name in vain.

[8] Remember the sabbath day, to keep it holy.

[12] Honour thy father and thy mother: that thy days may be long upon the land which the LORD thy God giveth thee.

[13] Thou shalt not kill.

[14] Thou shalt not commit adultery.

[15] Thou shalt not steal.

[16] Thou shalt not bear false witness against thy neighbor.

[**17**] Thou shalt not covet thy neighbor's house; thou shalt not covet thy neighbor's wife, nor his manservant, nor his maidservant, nor his ox, nor his ass, nor any thing that is thy neighbor's.

These words, allegedly from God, sound like scolding or ultimatums from a wrathful Parent telling a delinquent child what *not to do*. Remarkably, Divine counsel gives no guidance whatsoever on what *to do*, or more significantly *how to be*.

It is emotionally tantalizing to wonder how *we would be* or what may have happened had God addressed the Israelites not among clouds and thunder, smoke and fire, but rather on a remarkably sunny, cloud dappled day, with words such as:

[**1**] Thou shalt exalt in life and learn from the spectrum of experiences therein.

[**2**] In the entire universe, above all else, I hath chosen to express My divine heart and soul in Homo Divinitas and the life force of flora and fauna. All of life on earth share, each in their own way, the miracle of My creation.

[**3**] Thou shalt go forth and love thy sister and brother as I, for each is an expression of Me.

This author would like to attribute the following "Rules" to whoever wrote them but is unable to determine authorship. Nevertheless, the following ten rules are more spiritually wholesome that those allegedly delivered on Mount Sinai:

RULES FOR BEING HUMAN

[1] You will receive a body.

You may like it or hate it, but it will be yours for the entire period of this time around.

[2] You will learn lessons.

You are enrolled in a full-time informal school called Life. Each day in this school you will have the opportunity to learn lessons. You may like the lessons or think them irrelevant or stupid.

[3] There are no mistakes, only lessons.

Growth is a process of trial and error: Experimentation. The "failed" experiments are as much a part of the process as the experiment that ultimately "works".

[4] A lesson is repeated until learned.

A lesson will be presented to you in various forms until you have learned it. When you have learned it, you can go on to the next lesson.

[5] Learning lessons does not end.

There is no part of life that does not contain its lessons. If you are alive, there are lessons to be learned.

[6] "There" is no better than "here".

When your "there" has become a "here", you will simply obtain another "there" that will again look better than "here".

[7] Others are merely mirrors of you.

You cannot love or hate something about another person unless it reflects something you love or hate about yourself.

[8] What you make of your life is up to you.

You have all the tools and resources you need. What you do with them is up to you. The choice is yours.

[9] Your answers lie inside you.

The answers to Life's questions lie inside you. All you need to do is look, listen and trust.

[10] You will forget all this. (!)

This author is not aware of the intent of whoever wrote these rules and whether or not Rule #10 is facetious. Nevertheless, going one step further, it is provocative to suggest that these "rules"were at least a part of the homework assignment given to Homo Divinitas *prior* to incarnation…and yes, in that context, most of us have forgotten the first nine rules. Focusing on these rules of being will develop a more adequate inner awareness of self, and that which constitutes emotional fulfillment and self-esteem, as opposed to the repression and outright fear thrust down from the Mount at Sinai.

A way of developing strength of spirit in order to maximize self-esteem and thereby, insulate against fear and/or the emotional predator, would be the discipline of making choices that are spiritually fulfilling. Developing a reservoir of belief so as to determine, recognize, and deign pitfalls of emotional and moral quandary. Though not as threateningly as Moses, Pope Gregory the Great (ca. 540-604) decried seven "deadly" sins. "Sins" may better be referred to as character flaws because they lead to debilitation of spirit; they are, superbia (pride), invidia (envy), gula (gluttony), luxuria (extravagance, later lust), ira (wrath), avaritia (greed), and acedia (sloth).

Merriam-Webster defines pride as justifiable self-respect or haughty behavior: disdain. Both definitions are accurate. The first behavior is acceptable and to a certain extent, necessary. The second definition is the expression of flawed character. Disdain or haughty behavior is the expression of overcompensation of an insecure ego. There is freedom in not measuring one's self against other people because all people have strong and weak points and to focus on a weak point at any given moment disregards strengths not evident at a given moment. In most instances concerning differing points of view, one viewpoint may be more functional than another yet seldom are people totally "right" or totally "wrong". That being the case, generally speaking, people who are insecure, find solace in being "right" because "right" makes the other person "wrong", thus inferior. When two persons of an intimate relationship have a difference of opinion, they may "battle things out", or they may consider the context of their intimacy and understand that if one person is right the other becomes wrong. This may be, however is it so important to make the other person wrong? Revisiting Rochefoucauld once again, "A wise man thinks it more advantageous not to join the battle than to win." Certainly, a focus on any matter should be the mutual welfare of the participants however, in most cases, a liberal dose of understanding and compassion adds far more taste to the recipe of togetherness than the polarities of "right" and "wrong", winning and losing, subjugation and dominance.

The second "deadly" character flaw is envy. Envy: grudging desire for or discontent at the sight of another's excellence or advantages. Freedom from envy would entail focusing one's energy on one's own happiness, focusing on what one has as opposed to what one does not have. If Louis XVI of France, or Queen Victoria would be "beamed" from the 18th century to the 21st century of today, they would experience the wealth of convenience and standard of living beyond their wildest dreams. Virtually all of North America, Europe, and the economic powers of the Pacific Rim and Oceania enjoy air-conditioning or heating systems, refrigeration, electricity, telephones, radio, jet travel, plumbing and sewage, hot running water, shampoo, etc, *none* of which was available to monarchs of ages past. Yet, we are not happy with this cornucopia of convenience and luxury because we take them for granted or envy someone else for having more of them.

Quoting Democritus from Will Durant's *The Life of Greece*, "Happiness does not come from external goods; a man "must become accustomed to finding within himself the sources of his enjoyment." "Culture is better than riches...No power and no treasure can outweigh the extension of our knowledge." Happiness is fitful, and "sensual pleasure affords only a brief satisfaction"; one comes to a more lasting content by acquiring peace and serenity of soul (ataraxia), good cheer (euthumia), moderation (metriotes), and a certain order and symmetry of life (biou symmetria). We may learn much from the animals – "spinning from the spider, building from the swallow, singing from the nightingale and the swan"; but "strength of body is nobility only in beasts of burden, strength of character is nobility in man." So, like the heretics of Victorian England, Democritus raises upon his scandalous metaphysics a most presentable ethic. "Good actions should be done not out of compulsion but from conviction; not from hope of reward, but for their own sake.... A man should feel more shame in doing evil before himself than before all he world."[19]

Of like mind with Democritus in ancient Greece was his contemporary Antisthenes (444B.C. – 371B.C.). Antisthenes had this to say of envy, "As iron is eaten away by rust so the envious are consumed by their own passion." Democritus and Antisthenes were not Zen Buddhists yet remarkable it is that spiritual resonance can consistently be found within cross-cultural contexts.

People, in large part, refrain from focusing on inner spiritual being. Material possessions do not constitute happiness, if they did, royalty of eighteenth century Europe would envy the "commoner" of today. Because material possessions do not constitute happiness, "western" society is searching in the wrong places of emotional titillation, voyeurism and violence that dull the senses rather than enliven them. We live in an age of unparalleled ease, convenience, and wealth yet those selfsame "miracles" are ineffective if we do not derive happiness from them, and most do not. A man once starved is seldom, nay never displeased with a meal. If, on the other hand, someone visits India, a tourist would, in all likelihood be appalled by the apparent abject poverty amid the urban slums of Mumbai (Dharavi), Kolkata, even Agra (home of the Taj Mahal), or the rural poverty of thousands of smaller towns and villages. But upon closer scrutiny, when the traveler investigates below superficial material poverty, and thus begins to be acquainted with the people and their beliefs, one becomes acquainted with people of richness of spirit and one understands they are not concerned with what the tourist deems as poverty because people north and south of the Himalayas have, by and large a richness of community and spirit that guides their lives. Thus, "of life's two chief prizes, beauty and truth, I found the first in a loving heart and the second in a laborer's hand." – Khalil Gibran. The people of the Himalayas and Indian sub-continent are, for the most part (beggars notwithstanding) poor of wallet yet rich in spirit. The "west" on the other hand is rich of wallet and spiritually impoverished. Who is the wiser?

The third "deadly" character flaw is gluttony. Gluttony is the mirror image of envy. Gluttony is over-consumption of having. There is no rational need to consume more than one can use though egos and insecurity will try to convince otherwise. Gluttony is the irrational response to the need for material items to compensate for spiritual void.

Lust is the fourth "deadly" character flaw. Lust: sexual desire often to an intense or unrestrained degree. Intense sexual desire is appropriate however not when it exceeds the indeterminate boundary and becomes sexual gluttony. Emotions of affection are so formidably complex and within the duality of human existence (spirit and body) mankind wishes to express spiritual love through physical means. However the boundaries between love and lust are difficult to interpret. Please consider though that love enhances freedom, lust impairs it.

The fifth "deadly" character flaw is anger. The phrase goes," Someone else can make you angry, only with your permission". We have all heard someone say, "You make me so angry." In fact, anger is a subliminal condition of mind. Other people or situations serve only as catalysts for our own anger to trigger and thus become outwardly manifest. Just as people who have much beauty within, transpose that beauty on their environment, so do angry people always find cause to express anger. Were they not angry, anger would not have cause for expression. Personal freedom is enhanced by the recognition that each of us may express the choice to not participate in another person's anger. A peaceful state of mind is ceded when persons opt to participate in the anger of another. Egos may tell us that we must "make a point" but that does not mean reducing ones self to the malevolence of the other person. Besides, it is impossible to "win" an argument against the stubbornness of ignorance. Out-shouting or profanity demeans the user not the other party. What someone says or does and how someone reacts reflects his or her own karma.

Actions and reactions are a reflection of our own karma and well being, or lack thereof.

Greed is the "deadly" flaw that is selfish desire beyond reason. The illogical and unreasonable pursuit of 'more' is much the same as gluttony. Greed accomplishes only the acquisition of unnecessary items at the cost of freedom to follow reasonable needs.

Sloth is the last "deadly" sin. The corollary principle to sloth is that "the devil finds work for idle hands". It naturally follows that idle hands are idle when welfare is available. Welfare is beneficial when used as a safety net but detrimental when it becomes a hammock. When not pursuing necessity, mankind produces folly. We take pictures with cell-phones while thousands of people are starving in Darfur, Sudan, Africa. There is no causal relationship between these events yet one could ask why is there so little attention to Darfur when American teens (on behalf of their parents) spend hundreds of dollars for usage of cellular phones? It is ludicrous to suggest those societies preoccupied with cell phones and other techno-nauseam are causal to international neglect, much of which in the case of Darfur, Sudan is self-directed and continues unabated under the barbaric President Al-Bashir. Nevertheless, John Kenneth Galbraith was quoted in 1983 to have said, "I am struck by our superb capacity to manufacture consumer gadgetry, including electronic games, versus our capacity to produce schools." Had the astute Mr. Galbraith continued his comment he may well have said, "We have the capacity but lack the desire to build schools that will invest knowledge into future generations of children. In the economic superstructure of capitalism, profit is paramount." His remark as such does not refer to sloth yet if one looks closely enough, one can see that resources of society are for the most part, directed toward sating the pleasure urge, not in the pursuit of freedom or happiness.

Disconcerting it is to note that in a somewhat different context, Thomas More (1478-1535) predated Mr. Galbraith's observations five *centuries* earlier. Quoting from More's *Utopia*, (when expounding a view about contemporary England), "To make matters worse, this wretched poverty is most incongruously linked with expensive tastes. Servants, tradesmen, even farm-laborers, in fact all classes of society are recklessly extravagant about clothes and food. Then think how many brothels there are, including those that go under the names of wine-taverns or ale-houses. Think of the demoralizing games people play – dice, cards, backgammon, tennis, bowls, quoits – what are they but quick methods of wasting a man's money, and sending him straight off to become a thief?" If one juxtaposes ipod's, pda's (personal digital assistants) and camera cell-phones with dice, cards, et cetera, "The charm of history and its enigmatic lesson consist in the fact that, from age to age, nothing changes and yet everything is completely different." – Mr. Huxley.

As mentioned in *A New Reformation*, another set of "sins" were set forth by one of the great men of the twentieth century Mohandas K. Gandhi. These traits are, wealth without work, pleasure without conscience, science without humanity, knowledge without character, politics without principle, worship without sacrifice, and commerce without morality.

Biblical scripture renders the account of the crucifixion of Jesus. "The chief priests of the Jews protested to Pilate, "Do not write 'The King of the Jews', but that this man claimed to be king of the Jews." (John 19:21). Pilate refused and Jesus suffered corporeal death beneath the Latin inscription Iesvs Nazeranvs Rex Ivdaeorvm[f], hence the abbreviated INRI apparent on crosses of today that depict the appassionata of Christ. Assuming the accuracy of the account, this King, presumed or otherwise, did prior to his death, suffer immense pain under the only type of crown He would or ever could wear, a crown of thorns.

Homo Divinitas too, each one of us, bear a crown of thorns unto death. This is not to minimize in any way the thorns borne by Christ at the crucifixion for the physical pain must have been excruciating. However emotional and spiritual pain has a greater capacity to induce torment and despair. "An insincere and evil friend is more to be feared than a wild beast; a wild beast may wound your body, but an evil friend will wound your mind." – Buddha. These thorns are not as readily apparent yet are known to all as greed, envy, avarice, violence, hate, ad nauseum. Each of these thorns cause pain in this life, as did the crown of thorns bestowed upon Jesus prior to his death nailed upon Calvary's cross. His, and our crucifixion under thorn bear testimony to the honor and reverence that Homo Divinitas should render to himself, to others, and to different cultural renderings of the Godhead.

Whether moral principles and ethical behavior of honor and reverence are gleaned from scripture, philosophy or both, matters not. What matters is that we begin practicing those principles *now*. The time has come to emphasize love over hate, accountability and atonement over accusation and punishment, forgiveness over grudge, empathy over judgment, and tolerance over prejudice, brotherhood above all else. Love requires vulnerability and courage, accountability requires

---

[f] The "v" in Latin has become the anglicized "u". Whence the letter "vv" is now recognized as a "double-u"

honesty, forgiveness requires grace, empathy requires understanding, and tolerance requires patience. Courage, vulnerability, honesty, grace, understanding and patience, require the strength of virtue and right-mindedness. Until mankind rekindles, relearns, and practices these virtues in abundance, society will suffer the structural stresses born of weakness, those weaknesses being the wrong-mindedness of the pursuit of faux power, fear, and violence.

When structural engineers speak of stress, they speak of how much pressure any given material can sustain. A material can be subject to an allowable amount of stress and still essentially without effect, maintain its structural *integrity*. The greater the stress however, the more intense becomes the pressure that will compromise the *integrity* of the material. The material, or a structure from which it is built, becomes subject to collapse with evermore stress and pressure. A case can be made that the outlets of aggression, fear, and violence express stress and pressure of our global socio-economic environment. These negatives provide substantial stresses to the *integrity* of the social structure of mankind. Violence is the first option of personal weakness or ignorance.

Please consider the following anecdote regarding stress. An architect asked a client to lift a ream of paper and hold it at arms length. He then asked the client, "What is the weight of the paper?" The client responded, "I would say about 4 pounds." To whom the architect responded, "In a sense you are correct, but you are correct only for this moment. If moments are strung together for a longer period of time, does not the absolute weight of four pounds change to a weight which becomes unsustainable the longer you hold it at arms length?" The client recognized the accuracy of the statement and understood too, the self-applied philosophical ramifications of the scenario.

What exists now may not be as it seems and may certainly change as time elapses. A grudge held over a period of time is perhaps the world's heaviest burden, which ironically, affects only the grudger not the grudgee. Richard M. Nixon, in his farewell speech on August 9, 1974 when resigning his presidency remarked, "Always give your best, never get discouraged, never be petty; always remember others may hate you, but those who hate you don't win unless you hate them, and then you destroy yourself." One may ask when Mr. Nixon chanced upon, and began practicing this epiphany, nevertheless the veracity of his statement is emotionally unchallengeable.

Congruently, a professional baseball player can stand at home plate and hit an 80 mile-per-hour fastball with ease. A layperson never having played baseball would find that hitting the same pitch would be a daunting challenge. Skill levels notwithstanding, the speed of the 80-mph fastball, though being the same for each person, *seems* quite a different experience to each person. The same is true of the life experience. Life and circumstance occur at different rates and different intensities for different people. The manner in which life occurs is not necessarily right or wrong, good or bad, yet certainly in a unique way as determined by each individual. Relativity is present in Einstein's world of physics. Another type of relativity is present too in how we should consider ourselves vis-à-vis each other in that relativity. That which is negative for one may be positive for another. The 60's phrase, "Different strokes for different folks", comes to mind. Considering inconsistencies of occurrence, people would do well to acknowledge differences as applied to others, as they would expect others to respect differences in themselves. Should another person relate a story about a painful experience, it is inappropriate to discount their experience by commenting such as, "That's nothing compared to what I went through." To *them*, it is something! Their pain or happiness is real to them and is spoken not relative to the listener. Their experience of pain or joy is genuine, in and of itself. Their story is not meant as a referendum vis-à-vis the listener. Please have the courtesy to empathize and console or congratulate, whichever the case may be. Eventually each of us will find that we, and our feelings, will not be discounted because we will not discount other people. Insecure egos have a tendency to participate in one-ups-man-ship. Our arms are intended more for hugging others than ourselves.

The underlining aspect of the behavior of Homo Divinitas should be to emulate and learn from the positive examples before us. When we envy or hate other people, we consequently emotionally eviscerate ourselves in the process, and we become the victims of our own insecurity. The underlining aspect of Homo Divinitas must be to refocus the structure of our ethos of activity around ethical and moral principles that *do not change through time.* Homo Divinitas must take the extraordinary measure of recognizing the dimension of time for the mirage it is. At the turn of the 20th century, it was considered near scandalous behavior if a woman bared her ankle at the beach. Needless to say the passage of time has changed that perception. Please bear in mind that it wasn't the woman's body that was perceived as obscene, the only obscenity involved was our perception of her body.

Perceptions happen at an instant yet our interpretations of them change. To the extent we harbor obscenity or sadness we permit them to fester with the passage of time. Alfred Lord Tennyson (1809-1892) said, "A sorrows crown of sorrow is remembering happier times." We say, "time flies when you're having fun" and it does because we are unaware of time. "A watched kettle never boils" because we are too aware of time. Time passes quickly during sleep because we are not actively (consciously) participating in the illusion of time. Homo Divinitas must act to relieve the stresses and conflict in how we participate in the environment of time. We possess the ability to bequeath our own atonement. We must choose to exercise that atonement through forgiveness. We must be aware too, that time heals all wounds, *if we let them.*

Recently, a colleague of mine and I were watching television and a woman who, after being exposed to the disparaging remarks about the ladies of the Rutgers basketball team by radio host Don Imus, admitted she had been unaware of racial matters and apologized for being so. After her apology she also vowed to actively help others with racial understanding in her neighborhood. Upon hearing this statement, my colleague, a professing Christian, said aloud and with disdain words to the effect, "what took you so long…it's too late now (she was middle-aged). One wonders what reaction he might have had if, after finding Jesus as his Savior, God had said, "sorry, you're too late". His "faith" has not helped him to identify with forgiveness or to assuage the pain in his heart. Quoting the British Statesman Benjamin Disraeli (1804-1881), "Grief is the agony of an instant. The indulgence of grief the blunder of a life."

Time may, if improperly perceived, further daunt a person's spiritual welfare and emotional wholeness. The following quotes prove this principle yet they do so coming from different angles. "Fear is pain arising from the anticipation of evil" – Aristotle. And concurrently with the modern era, "Worry is interest paid on a debt you may never owe." Freedom exists in the non-attachment to time.

There is no happiness in perpetuation of violence and conflict. We must realize (make real) forgiveness and brotherhood. That selfsame forgiveness and brotherhood is healthiest when self-applied. The phrase is heard, "He is his own worst enemy." Why should this be so? And, "perfectionism is the sincerest form of self-abuse." It is not necessary to be better than someone else however the case can be made that it is always necessary to do one's best. If someone has not performed to the best of their ability they may be subject to the tendency for doubt, regret, and guilt. One seldom has a second opportunity to make a good first impression. The disease of self-inflicted agony manifests by means of the fulcrum of time. Guilt, happiness, reprieve, or angst are predicated on the 'IF' (outcome) of *future* events, or disillusion with results of *past* events. **If** an outcome is immediately advantageous and/or pleasurable, the result is viewed and accepted as positive. **If** an outcome is deleterious or disadvantageous results may well be interpreted as negative, yet perspectives change with the passage of time. Events are seldom as good or as bad as they seem. We tend to chastise ourselves when, in any given circumstance, one choice is made, then in retrospect (hindsight is 20/20) wish the other. Second-guessers are correct solely because they determined the right answers after the test results were published! Soren Kierkegaard's quote mentioned earlier is appropriate once again, "Life can only be understood backwards but it must be lived forwards." There are few philosophers among us with the acumen of Mr. Kierkegaard nevertheless it does not take a philosopher's mind to realize that the *first* person to criticize after the fact would also be the *last* person not to provide counsel before the fact. Only those who are emotionally insecure use fate as a way to bludgeon with guilt, choices originally made in earnest. Insecure persons of weak esteem will attempt to use the imaginary "if" to try to construct an imaginary wisdom after-the-fact in order to undermine the emotional welfare of a decision maker by taunting them if a decision is perceived as being 'wrong'. People who are insecure will construct "*if's*" solely to afford the opportunity to say, "I told you so" and are motivated by no other reasons than insecurity and/or envy. People who are insecure may say to a perceived "offender", "What if *everybody* did that?" knowing full well than everybody *won't* do that! This tactic is an immature expression of nonsense used to reinforce a position when logic cannot be applied.

A more sinister manifestation of the occult concept of "if" exists when "if" masquerades as hope behind the mask of chance, i.e. gambling. Gambling is an attempt to gain something by doing nothing (other than tempting risk vis-à-vis "reward"), parlaying hope for money. The word "usury" is derived from the Medieval Latin *usuria* meaning "interest". "Usury", through the centuries, has been permitted to mean "excessive interest". Ancient leaders such as Aristotle, Cicero, Plato, Aquinas, Moses, the prophet Mohammed, and Buddha denounced usury. Usuria, or interest, was considered morally reprehensible by philosophy and scripture alike because something of value was created without being earned (i.e. the creation of financial capital). Should a lender provide 10 shekels for thirty days and demand payment of 12 shekels, the lender realizes 2 shekels of interest gained by leveraging time against the borrower, and time is solely within the province of God. Consequently, the 2 shekels gleaned from the borrower are considered ill gotten, thus sinful.

Gambling is usurious to the extreme because gambling betrays "hope". Should someone win a bet, they lose because they have obtained something earned by effort that is counterfeit. Should someone lose a bet, they have sold their "hope" and received nothing. When Dante described the inscription over the Gates of Hell in his enduring classic *Inferno*, he chose these words, "Lose hope, all ye who enter here." Yet people eagerly sell hope in vast quantities. In most cases, government sanctions if not permits this insidious activity. State-sponsored gambling (Lotto) permits politicians to add another source of tax revenue without calling it a tax! On a national level, the Securities and Exchange Commission regulates gambling however the SEC refers to equity and futures activity on the floors of America's bourses as "trading" not gambling! And, win, lose, or draw, financial brokers receive a rake (commission) just like bookies!

Those who determine actuarial tables in any given commercial/ financial equation, always set (tip) the scales so they win (profit), at the expense of the clientele they profess to serve. People who manufacture "odds" and reap financial commission on outcomes of future events do so by projecting occultisms on what may or may not happen. "If" the Fightin' Irish lose, I win! Or better yet, if you buy Enron stock you'll be rich! Outside the sporting arena, the "odds" mentality arises in the perennial question, "what are my chances?" The fact of the matter is that there are no "odds" to any event however people who are perceived to be able to delve such things are asked to create pseudo-odds in order to mollify the questioner. Manipulative persons of less than altruistic motive may try to induce or seduce the curious, insecure, or anxious so they may profit from the premise of hope or insecurity of doubt. The questions "what are the odds?" or "what are my chances?" can be answered in only one way The fact is that there are only two outcomes to any given event. The "odds" are 100% that something will happen or it will not, *only time will tell*. What were the "odds" that the undefeated Ohio State Buckeyes would amass only 83 yards of total offense in the 2007 Bowl Championship Series championship game against the Florida Gators? The answer is 100% because it happened, yet odds-makers offer "odds" before the fact so they can profit at the expense of those who vainly attempt to gain something for nothing. Odds-makers or emotional predators offer gamblers and/or those insecure persons the opportunity to place bets of financial and/or emotional consequence based on the illusion of possibility of future happenstance to usurp riches that the gullible or insecure, willingly or in the case of addiction, involuntarily cede. Xanadu of the desert, Las Vegas, is a testimonial to the success of the sideshow barker... step right this way, have I got a deal for you!

The loss of self-esteem and consequently freedom, comes into play when persons weak of spirit, succumb to jealous attempts at condemnation by emotional predators who try to bring others down to his or her level. Quantitative terms such as right and wrong, when used to describe opinions or choices may well be inappropriate. When an individual expresses a point of view and another person shares the same viewpoint, the first impulse is to say, "You're right". In fact, the correct terminology would be "I agree", or "we are in accord". In fact, two people can both be mistaken and still be in accord, they just both agree on the same fallacious viewpoint. Viewpoints can be valid or not valid without necessarily being "right" or "wrong". Opposing viewpoints can be valid and coexistent when they are not polarized with terms such as "right" or "wrong". All events occur as they should and all outcomes are as they should be.

Robotic assumption of the negative is self-flagellation of which we should have no participation. No reason exists other than predisposed self-applied negativity to assume the worst and use it *against* ourselves. A case in point, "Yes, I took the San Bernardino freeway, and yes, I'm stalled in traffic, and I'm mad! *If* only I had taken the Pomona Freeway, I'd be better off! We assume *if* we had made another choice, and *if* all else remained equal, the other choice would have been better. To assume all other things would remain equal is fallacious. Perhaps the silent angels who guide our actions put me on the San Bernardino Freeway because *if* I had chosen the Pomona Freeway I would have been in a serious accident.

Assuming the negative by constructing a self-destructive "if-scenario" is like practicing self-voodoo with needles of doubt and pain. We do not know why events occur so we should not presume to create "if-scenarios" that virtually always assume the negative and use it to anguish others and ourselves. Insecure, petulant egos make these assumptions in order to justify egoic existence. "If" is a mirage. Only "is" is, and "is" lasts only for a moment! A world of difference exists between "is" and "if." Emotional right-mindedness requires a person to accept the divinity and perfect condition of the creation that "is" understanding that felicity and adversity are the keys of the same piano from which the harmony of life is comprised. Each defines the other, and the wise of heart and soul learn from one as from the other. Thomas Carlyle reminds us that, "adversity is the diamond dust Heaven polishes its jewels with." This is not to say that we should not make efforts to minimize misfortune and hardship, we should. But in fact, the journey toward wellness of *spiritus mundi* would be to eliminate violence and hate and understand that felicity and adversity define our realm of being and each define the blessings of the other. Within the realm of present reality, such as we understand it to be, the first step in doing so is to recognize that we, each of us, must be the agent of change toward a *spiritus mundi* of ethical and moral direction.

Another adage states "you really appreciate something only after you lose it". If that is the agreement one decides to realize, to make real, so be it. That aside, one may learn from the Angel of Death. Quoting from *The Four Agreements: A Toltec Wisdom*, "The final way to attain personal freedom is to prepare ourselves for the initiation of the dead; to take death itself as our teacher. What the Angel of Death can teach us is how to be truly alive. We become aware that we can die at any moment. We have just the present to be alive. The fact is that we don't know if we are going to die tomorrow. Who knows? We have the idea that we have many years in the future, but do we? If we go to the hospital and the doctor tells us that we have one week to live, what are we going to do? As we have mentioned before, we have two choices. One is to suffer because we are going to die and to tell everyone "Poor me, I am going to die" and really create a huge drama. The other choice is to use every moment to be happy. To do what we really enjoy doing. If we only have one week to live, let's enjoy life. Let's be alive. We can say, "I'm going to be myself. No longer am I going to run my life trying to please other people. No longer am I going to be afraid of what they think about me. What do I care what others think if I'm going to die in one week. I'm going to be myself". The Angel of Death can teach us to live every day as if it is the last day of our life as if there may be no tomorrow. We can begin each day by saying, "I am awake. I see the sun. I'm going to give my gratitude to the sun and to everything and everyone because I'm still alive. One more day to be myself." That is the way I see life. That is what the Angel of Death taught me. To be completely open, to know that there is nothing to be afraid of. And of course, I treat the people I love with love because this may be the last day that I can tell you how much I love you."[20] Life and death are not opposites. Birth and death are opposites, and as such, are the two greatest miracles of creation. Life has no opposite life is eternal.

Positing further, one can be thankful not merely for blessings of happiness but for the unanticipated despair, hurt or tragedy that does **not** happen. How many persons who eat three square meals a day take each of those meals for granted without being truly thankful for the abundance at the table, and the ease with which it was obtained? The point of the exercise is that we are able to *choose* whether or not to be thankful for life's abundances. Starvation is not necessary in order to be thankful for a meal. Do not wait to lose an arm before being thankful for having two. If one waits to do so, it's already too late. A person may, at the end of the day be grateful he or she was **not** involved in an automobile accident, or they may not. One can be thankful for the use of their limbs or they can choose **not** to be. One can rue the loss of eyesight or choose to see beauty through the unprejudiced eye of the mind. The quality of existence is determined by the sum of our choices and the values we select to define choice. Callousness and joy, benevolence and selfishness, morality and immorality exist so as to give Homo Divinitas a palette with which he may paint a portrait of despair or triumph.

PART TWO
THE JOURNEY

CHAPTER 6
THE NATURE OF CONFLICT

"Anger is an acid that can do more harm to the vessel in which it is stored than to anything on which it is poured."
– Mark Twain (1835-1910).

The nature of conflict can be defined as the intellectual and/or emotional (and perhaps subsequently, physical) friction between two or more parties, at least one of whom is an aggressor. Aggression usually takes the form of pushing (applying forceful pressure) by physical and/or emotional means. None other than Leonardo da Vinci voiced an insightful observation regarding the relationship between man's physiology and man's behavior. da Vinci said, "The function of muscle is to pull and not to push except in the case of the genitals and the tongue."

How extraordinary that da Vinci made the distinction between these two muscles and their capacity for aggression. Anatomically (internally) muscles work in concert to accomplish a given task by *pulling* in the same direction. Socially (externally) we may choose to pull someone toward us, which essentially is the action of a caress, or hug. Socially, potential strife and conflict is caused by *pushing* (shoving) at each other with our tongues (language) driven by psyche (ego), or unwanted sexual advance driven by libido expressed through genitalia. Libido is more pliant than ego and sexual tension when accompanied by the enjoyment of mutual climax is the most sublime expression of intimacy between Homo Divinitas. However, people seldom benefit from conflict even though their egos seek conflict as a reason for self-justification and self-perpetuation (I am right and you are wrong). A "winner" and "loser" may arise from any conflict nevertheless both or all participants of conflict bear painful physical and/or emotional scars. And…time may change the perception of the outcome, so are the mental and emotional scars of justification worth the pain?

Right and wrong are matters of manipulation and relativity. The June 10, 1991 issue of TIME magazine ran an article entitled *Evil* by Lance Morrow. The article asked the question, "Does evil exist?" Quoting from that article, "Evil is anyone outside the tribe. Evil works by dehumanizing the Other. A perverse, effective logic: identifying others as evil justifies all further evil against them. A man may kill a snake without compunction. The snake is an evil thing, has evil designs, is a different order of being. Thus: an "Aryan" could kill a Jew, could make an elaborate bureaucratic program of killing Jews. Thus: white men could come in the middle of the night in Mississippi and drag a black man out and hang him. Getting people to think in categories is one of the techniques of evil. Marxist-Leninist zealots thought of "the bourgeoisie," a category, a class, not the human beings, and it is easy to exterminate a category, a class, a race, an alien tribe.

Mao's zealots in the Cultural Revolution, a vividly brainless evil, destroyed China's intellectual classes for a generation. Pol Pot's Khmer Rouge sent to the killing fields all who spoke French or wore glasses or had soft hands. The Khmer Rouge aimed to cancel all previous history and begin at Year Zero. Utopia, this century has learned the hard way, usually bears a resemblance to hell. An evil chemistry turns the dream of salvation into damnation."[21] The "west" is an evil tribe, the "Great Satan". British author Rudyard Kipling (1865-1936) had his own viewpoint on the 'tribe'. "The individual has always had to struggle to keep from being overwhelmed by the tribe. To be your own man is a hard business. If you try it, you will be lonely often, and sometimes frightened. But no price is too high to pay for the privilege of owning yourself." Mr. Kipling interestingly enough, had the singleness of identity to refuse both British knighthood and Poet Laureateship. Mr. Kipling, knowingly or not, followed the lead of Buddha, "It is better to conquer yourself than to win a thousand battles. Then the victory is yours. It cannot be taken from you, not by angels or by demons, heaven or hell."

When pondering the privilege of owning yourself, consider these observations about "tribes". For the most part, religions of the east are primarily systems of belief. Conversely, the missionary religions such as Christianity and Islam focus not on belief so much as behavior or conduct. Buddhism of Gautama Siddhartha or Taoism of Lao Tzu counsel on enlightenment and right-mindedness, which is to say the essence of emotional purity. Though Christianity places much emphasis on John 3:15, "That whosoever believeth in Him shall not perish but have everlasting life", much emphasis is also placed on James 2:26, "For as the body without the spirit is dead, so faith without works is dead also." The rending of spiritual expression into schools of religious theology serves to provide yet another category that divides the human family of Homo Divinitas. "Tribe", on whatever level, determines a we/they concept. "We/they" without an ethos of understanding and egalitarianism virtually always leads to domination/suppression as expressed in conflict between races, Christian or Muslim, believer or heathen, fat or slender, rich or poor, republican or democrat, Yankee fan or Red Sox fan, Sunni or Shia, beautiful or ugly, that serve to polarize society not unite it. Incidentally, ugliness exists only when describing actions not appearances. Should someone say words to the effect "you are ugly", the comment is a revealing one however the comment speaks volumes about the speaker not the person to whom it is intended. The few ugly people in this world are those who would say such a thing. Again quoting Rudyard Kipling. "All the people like us are we, and everyone else is they."

Recently, in France, a woman who had been seriously injured was surgically given a new face. This serves to reinforce that one's face is only a convenient mode of recognition for the soul it represents. Facial features and/or body type or color has *nothing* to do with the essence of who we *are*. A name is a convenient form of identification that serves to facilitate practical matters of societal function however; names have *nothing* to do with who we *are*. Our skin provides a packaging system to contain organs and muscles however the color of the packaging has *nothing* to do with who we *are* any more than what type of wrapping is used for presents under a Christmas tree.

Who we are is determined by what we do and how we treat others and ourselves. Outward physical differences conceal the sameness of purpose we all share. We wish to experience freedom of body and soul, to raise or children so they may experience a more fulfilling life than their parents. We wish to sleep without hunger and yearn for the blessing of experiencing true love. Efforts by politicians to tribalize in the realms of governance and religion serve to confuse and obfuscate the family of Homo Divinitas into sectarian and religious conflict. One can only speculate when we became we/they, though at least biblically speaking, Cain and Abel can provide an example of sorts. Nevertheless, because this condition has always been so does not mean it must remain so. It may remain so only should we continue to provide such permission. Homo Divinitas must become the change we envision and desire; each one of us! If politics is removed from governance, we subsequently lose identification with and relations to, geographical boundaries, passports, and flags. In so doing, we become one step closer to being a family. If politics is removed from worship, we subsequently lose identification with and relations to a wrathful, judgmental Deity consequently Homo Divinitas gains the unfettered opportunity to acknowledge Divinity as we freely determine. Quoting the English philosopher John Stuart Mill (1806-1813), "Whatever crushes individuality is despotism, by whatever name it may be called and whether it professes to be enforcing the will of God or the injunctions of men." If this sort of ethos seems unattainable, this is so only because we have been negatively programmed to choose to understand it as such. Self-limitation occurs when we accept limits, when we realize limits.

When a baby elephant is born into a village in India, it represents an asset to the village. To insure the new arrival does not stray, as young ones are wont to do, a large iron bracelet is placed around an ankle on a rear leg. The bracelet has a stake attached and is pounded into the ground whenever the baby elephant needs to be kept from wandering. Naturally the baby wants to roam and will strain against the shackle but he will not be able to free himself. Consequently the little elephant resigns himself to the restricted area he has been allotted. This mindset remains the same throughout the elephant's life. As a fully-grown adult, the elephant will more than quadruple in size and strength and could use that domesticating stake for a toothpick, however the elephant does not know he can do so because **he thinks he can't.**

This author believes in miracles. I have witnessed them in person though my definition of what constitutes a miracle or a miracle-worker may be somewhat different than most. A miracle was the survival of my daughter who was born 24 weeks after conception and weighed only 21 ounces. I have witnessed angels doing miracles when I see families returning from overseas with an adopted child. I see an angel working miracles every day when I see my wife administering a program for the local school district that avails assistive technologies to open the world of wonder, learning, and communication to children in dire need of understanding, care, and love. I am reminded of the angels who acted in first response performing myriad miracles of heroism in New York, Washington D.C., and rural Pennsylvania on a fateful day in 2001. Within each of us lies the uncommon courage of common people. Is it not ironic that when each of us, at the caprice of circumstance, rises to the level of heroic behavior, that most angels express humility when speaking of the essence of that selfsame courage?

The journey to the top of the mountain will have moments of challenge that provide opportunity for the common man or woman to exercise uncommon courage. The fittest of salmon survive only because they had the determination or inner drive to overcome the current of the river. The view from the mountaintop of brotherhood and serenity is extraordinarily beautiful. However one, and only one obstacle prevents civilizations from achieving the vista, a pandemic of apathy. Apathy and/or negative thought are self-inflicted anesthesia of spirit. We have the courage, latent or otherwise, to break the coma of spirit however we must *realize* courage, i.e. make it real. A mountain climb begins with the first step. A first step may be a random act of kindness asking no recompense. It may begin with the trust of a handshake or a pat on the back. Positive emotions, positive thoughts, positive reasons and determination will change the world if we *realize* them. A tidal wave consists of billions of drops of water moving in one direction. A tidal wave of change may occur when each of mankind strives to reach an ideal of mutual benefit with positive momentum of brotherhood and togetherness. We not we/ they. One letter makes a world of difference between the meaning of the words "if" and "is", so too with the words "me" and "we". "Me" becomes "we" when selfishness is eschewed. When people disdain selfishness, we help ourselves. If you (pardon first person) commit to helping others, please consider the possibilities of millions of other people simultaneously doing the same. By so doing, millions of people are committing to help you. We must become the world we envision. What matters most is the cultivation of the awareness of our selves not as one drop of water, but as one wave.

Neo-Platonism of ancient Greek philosophy taught that God is a Supreme, Infinite Being. Plotinus (204-270 CE), considered the founder of the Neo-Platonic school believed that creation was a continual process of the Creator with each creational wave somewhat diminished from the last. Plotinus deemed the first creative wave as Nous (Divine mind) enabling God to contemplate God, thus establishing awareness of Divine Being, though by nature, no longer a unitary entity. The succeeding creational wave created Psyche as the world soul[g] (spiritus mundi). Significance lies in the view that Psyche,

---

[g] please see *A New Reformation: Spirituality and the Politics of Organized Religion*, by this author.

as presented in Neo-Platonist thought, represented an entity unto itself though fragmented into separate souls. The Neo-Platonists may have been the first western school of thought to acknowledge that we are all as one Divine entity, one wave. And, revisiting the Divine nature of artistic expression, drawing a parallel with the proverbial sound in the forest, Nous thus would be understood as Divinity, recognizing, creating, and loving the art form of Man qua Divinity.

As a sidebar, it is interesting to note that another proponent of Neo-Platonism was Hypatia (370-415CE) of Alexandria. Hypatia, a formidable intellect in her own right was a North-African contemporary of Augustine. Being a woman though, she was dealt with more severely than Pelagius. Whereas Pelagius was excommunicated and exiled for his heretic thought, Christian Bishop Cyril apparently had his monks strip her, beat her, and burn her body. Fortunately for Hypatia, she apparently was not raped, because these were monks, after all. Mysogyny – the hatred of women. Hypatia was honored by the genius Raphael when he included Hypatia (along with Aristotle, Plato, Diogenes, Heraclites, among others) in his masterpiece, The School of Athens. The scatological behavior and neurotic thought of Bishop Cyril, Augustine, Tertullian, Irenaeus, et al, live with us today.

Quoting Carl Jung, "The meeting of two personalities is like the contact of two chemical substances. If there is any reaction, both are transformed." Consider the importance of the word "reaction" in its context. Homo Divinitas must summon wisdom and courage not to *react* to, participate in, and thus create alchemy with those who espouse terror, fear, and hatred. Helen Keller, an angel to be sure, is quoted in *A New Reformation*, "It is wonderful how much time good people spend fighting the devil. If they would only expend the same amount of energy loving their fellow men, the devil would die in his own tracks of ennui." In this context, it matters not whether evil manifests itself as the devil or in religious zealots behaving like the devil. This is not to say that western civilization must become prostrate before the scythe of violence of extremist Islam, however the most effective way of coping with violence is to *isolate* not *react*. Societies should cope with the emotional disease of religious terror the same way societies manage epidemics of physical disease, with a quarantine of isolation to prevent contagion. Reaction merely serves to metastasize hate into virulent confrontation. Challenge those of violence with ideas rather than join them in an orgy of blood. Wisdom, courage and humility are among other values, expressions of the divine endowment to Homo Divinitas. Wisdom, courage, humility are strengths that will overpower weakness such as ignorance and emotional poverty. Those who are able can recognize wisdom in the following quote by W.B. Prescott, "In any contest between power and patience bet on patience."

We are prisoners of the finite states of length, width, and height, yet with patience can we conquer time. "Everything comes gradually and at its appointed hour." – Ovid. To the extent each of us can strive for wisdom, exercise courage in word and deed, and yet remain humble, each of us can embrace a spark of Divinity, thereby becoming an angel striving toward the end of tribalism (we/they). In fact we are *one family* of the Great Integrity. This is Homo Divinitas of whom I speak.

Scatological behavior of international terrorists and their amoral counterparts in the political arenas of governance and religion, who choose to lower themselves to the lowest common denominator lusting for power and influence, serve to diminish the privilege of self-ownership. Mohandas Karamchand Gandhi was the conscience behind the movement that wrought what is now India, formerly British India. The Mahatma (Sanskrit for Great Soul) thundered against the might, weapons, and pedestrian yet tyrannical rule of the British Empire with the moral imperative of Satyagraha, the resistance of tyranny through mass civil disobedience, firmly founded upon ahimsa or total non-violence. The strength and prodigious moral courage of Mohandas K. Gandhi led to home-rule (independence from the British Empire) for the nation of India. He chose not to stoop to the barbarity of the British power brokers and the world continues to pay homage to his moral brilliance. His virtuous moral might was so compelling that he and his followers broke the chains of domination not with force, but with courage, not with anger, but with determination. In this realm dwell those of truest strength. Tragically, Gandhi paid the ultimate price for his courage as did thousands of his countrymen, yet his (and their) epitaphs is written with honor and determination not hate and cowardice.

Khan Abdul Ghaffar Khan (1890-1988) was a Pashtun political and spiritual leader also known for non-violence. Ghaffar Khan was born and lived most of his entire life in Peshawar, North-West Frontier Province, British India (subsequently Pakistan). A Muslim contemporary of Gandhi's, Khan too was recognized for his moral courage. He was also known as Badshah Khan, "King of Chiefs". Khan was so known because he, as Gandhi, sought a free, united, and secular India and founded Khudai Khidmatgar (Servants of God) to that end. Ghaffar Khan advised its members, "I am going to give you such a weapon that the police and the army will not be able to stand against it. It is the weapon of the Prophet, but you are not aware of it. That weapon is patience and righteousness. No power on earth can stand against it."

The tyranny of Soviet communism succumbed to the German people when the Berlin Wall crumbled under the patient power and inertia of their desire for freedom. The wisdom of Leo Tolstoy once again, "The two most powerful warriors are patience and time." Power can be outflanked by the gentle finesse of wisdom, albeit with patience and determination. The process will last longer but the foundation will be a firm one. Contrary to Machiavelli, inspiring respect is more effective than causing fear. Virtue and honesty are hallmarks of a Statesman, expediency and demagoguery are tools of convenience for the politician weak in spirit, strong in desire. Former United States Secretary of State and presidential advisor Henry Kissinger has said, "Power is the ultimate aphrodisiac." Those who consider power an aphrodisiac are those *least* qualified to wield power.

Terrorists of the last forty years are little more than counterfeit, impotent, selfish moral imposters who have not knowledge, integrity, patience, wisdom, or discipline, who commit cowardly acts of religi-homicide so they can sleep with seventy virgins. Martyrdom is a handshake with the devil if the only reason for martyrdom is suicide by religion. Revisiting Kierkegaard once again, "The difference between a man who faces death for the sake of an idea and an imitator who goes in search of martyrdom is that the former expresses his idea most fully in death while the latter really enjoys the bitterness of failure." The cowardly act of giving up on life (and taking the lives of others in so doing) because their quality of life is rife with misery, despair, and ignorance is morally repugnant. To quote Rudyard Kipling once again, "Borrow trouble for yourself, if that's your nature, but don't lend it to your neighbors." Gandhi's moral courage and honor will be revered forever. A measure of transcendent immortality is when a person's goodness is remembered by family and loved ones, a community or village, a nation, or society at large. Gandhi's pathetic assassin/coward is already forgotten.

"Bugsy" Siegel (born Benjamin Siegelbaum, 1906-1947) was the mobster visionary (prophet?) who foresaw, in his mind, what was to become the epitome of excess, Las Vegas, Nevada. When pitching the idea to the likes of Meyer Lansky and "Lucky" Luciano, he was reportedly to have said words to the effect that, "build it and they will come." In the same manner when the Prophet promised houris (virgins) and a garden of delight (heaven, *Jannat*), is it any wonder that there is no dearth of recruits for jihad? The promise of riches, whether in this life or the next, shares the same common denominator of violent death whether for Bugsy or a jihadi. Today's religi-bombers self-annihilate like so much chaff before the scythe of fanatic polemicists who manipulate idealism and ignorance. Martyrdom is reserved for those who **preserve** rather than **destroy** life.

Militarily speaking, it is virtually always strategically advantageous to maintain the high ground. Politicians who muster national armed forces do so in order to gain military superiority through force of arms. Until now, leaders have chosen to enforce national policy by marshalling their force of military arms. Morally bereft politicians of the world stage perpetuate the global condition of violence when they choose to become part of it by reinforcing politically expedient policy by force and in so doing cede the *moral* high ground. In a war between two barbarians, it matters not who is the victor.

The United States in particular, and for that matter, Western Civilization in general, is involved in conflict with the more radical elements of the world of Islam and their "weapons of mass destruction". Supposedly it matters how one defines the term however one may wish to consider that any bomb that has ever been dropped should be considered a weapon of mass destruction. People who participated in World War II and Viet Nam can testify to that. Any automatic or semi-automatic weapon is a weapon of mass destruction. The definition merely differs depending upon the tribe to which one belongs. Not to defend the politico-religious barbarism of the Middle East but consider that the United States is the only country that has *used* the atomic bomb against a populace. Yes, we are all familiar with the reasons for doing so, yet virtually anything can be justified if one digs deep enough. The "west" rails against Hezbollah and Al-Qaida and rightly so, yet stooping to their level debases us in the process. "The lust for power is not rooted in strength, but in weakness." – Erich Fromm. Intimidation manifests in large part not because of the strength of the aggressor so much as in the weakness of lack of self-esteem and assuredness of the intended target.

Geography reduces the following question to a hypothetical basis because, unlike Israel, the United States has non-aggressive relations with its neighbors. That being the case, consider a scenario that would involve the invasion of the United States by an unfriendly force. Might the N.R.A. (National Rifle Association) constitute a type of Hezbollah? The answer is just as hypothetical as the question because the United States has a strong and established military force that includes reserve units. The point to be made is that aggression is the result of ignorance. Our populace has availability to any number of automatic weapons. Irony lies in the fact that anyone in possession of a gun is a potential terrorist! The difference is that our citizen militia has not had occasion to use ours *yet*. The cycle of violence will remain until men such as Sadat and Begin once again grace the world stage.

The world's political arena is filled with persons who simultaneously possess political genius and moral impotence. In ancient times, rulers would have concubines available for personal pleasure. Men who were sexually impotent or men who were castrated were selected to guard and supervise the purity of the harem. Such men were referred to as eunuchs. An emperor would keep a large harem in order to reinforce his masculinity and to insure heirs would survive (in an era of high infant mortality) to inherit the power of the throne. The term "eunuch" most often referred to an emasculated man yet not exclusively so. "Eunuch" is derived from two Greek words, "eune" (bed), and "ekhein" (to keep), i.e. "bed keeper" or "bed holder". The ruler's castrati were considered merely placeholders. Eunuchs were not the real thing however; they were regarded as being beyond reproach or temptation. With the passage of time, the term "eunuch" referred to those who were entrusted with oversight of treasuries or matters of secret consequence. Ergo, a regent with a legion of trusted eunuchs could delegate sundry matters and concentrate on amassing and maintaining power and rule.

This concept is a provocative one that bears closer scrutiny. It would be naïve to assume that rulers, concubines, and eunuchs do not exist today. They do exist, however not in the form they took in ages past. Rulers, concubines, and castrati populate corporate boardrooms, director's suites, the West Wing, and other venues of power and influence. The aspirations, motivations, and role of the ruler remain unchanged. Those who bed any stranger, and/or compromise any value, to accumulate power and/or wealth at any cost, play the role of concubine. Eunuchs are those of intellectual and/or emotional means who choose to be yes-men or withhold principled dissent and in so doing choose the self-castration of moral impotence. One must remember that, then as now, if eunuchs were required to insure the purity of the harem, it would be the *members of the harem who were untrustworthy*! Rulers who thirst of the allure of power without regard to convention, virtue, or morality contained in the free exchange of ideas and philosophy rely on subservient concubines to share their lust and the silence of the lambs, the impotent eunuchs, to turn a blind moral eye to their sordid affairs.

The world in conflict struggles to find political solutions and has completely failed to address issues honestly and forthrightly. Political solutions are as morally contaminated as the politicians who construct them. In the realm of politics, facts are bypassed, results are "spun", "right" and "wrong" are subject to interpretation, and insecure egos engage on the battlefield of righteousness while sacrificing the lives of innocents to reinforce their perception of "right". If politicians felt so compelled in their commitment to principle, why do they not vouchsafe their own cause, instead of doing so by cowardly delegation? Several generations ago, English author H.G. Wells asked, "Is it not reasonable that those who gamble with men's lives should not pay with their own?" Mr. Wells' question remains as yet unanswered. The bully's of the world stage, whether they be named Kim Jung-Il, Robert Mugabe, Ehud Olmert, Fidel Castro, Osama bin-Ladin, George W. Bush, Omar al-Bashir, or other heads of state whose incumbency mean more than the honor of standing for principle all have the blood of innocent people on their hands and the consequences of destructive karma bearing on their souls. Politics is antithetical to Truth.

Conflict in the world of sports pits opponents against each other, each of whom seek victory. The basic premise of sports is to score points in order to vanquish the opponent. This is a type of vicarious combat. Competition, on the field or off, is natural and appropriate if, and only if, the wisdom of Grantland Rice is remembered, "For when the One Great Scorer comes to write against your name, He marks – not that you won or lost – but how you played the game." When Arthur Wellesley, Duke of Wellington claimed that "the battle of Waterloo was won on the playing fields of Eton", he wasn't referring to their won-lost record. His words were a testimony to the development of discipline in applying uncompromising excellence to physical and intellectual endeavor. After winning at all cost, that which endures is not victory but the cost of victory. In the context of the continuum of perpetual time, the victor in turn becomes the vanquished at the hands of the next victor and subsequently, that which remains is not perpetual victory but perpetual cost of perpetual conflict. What lingers is a legacy of suffering and pain.

Quoting Zbigniew Brzezinski[h] regarding perpetual cost, "Thus during the twentieth century, no less than 167,000,000 lives – and quite probably in excess of 175,000,000 – were deliberately extinguished through politically motivated carnage. That is the approximate equivalent of the total population of France, Italy, and Great Britain; or over two-thirds of the total current population of the United States. This is more than the total killed in *all* previous

---

[h] Mr. Brzezinski was National Security Advisor in the Carter Administration (1977-1981) and is Professor of American Foreign Policy at Johns Hopkins University.

wars, civil conflicts, and religious prosecutions throughout human history. These horrendous though dry numbers are also a reminder of what can happen when humanity's innate capacity for aggression becomes harnessed by dogmatic self-righteousness and is enhanced by increasingly potent technologies of destruction."[22] The chilling aspect of the beginning of the twenty-first century seems to be that we have learned little from the bloodshed of the twentieth. The litany of violence and agony continues in Iraq in particular, the middle east in general, and Afghanistan, Myanmar, Sudan, Sri Lanka, ad nauseum. With all the advancements and refinements borne of the industrial age, the technological age, and the information age, has life become any easier or more comfortable? In many respects the answer is yes. Yet it should be rather evident at this point in the metamorphosis of mankind that any gains on a material level have had virtually no positive effect of the malaise of spirit of man. The condition of spititus mundi will forever dwell in a state of what Buddhism refers to as samodaya (spiritual longing) until we have the wisdom to deign power and wealth and have the courage to love and forgive, to focus on spiritual fulfillment over material riches. With all the technologies and information available, we have not yet learned to solve the equation of human need. Human needs are best met when we realize that ego is the imposter of self, that we stand tallest when we stoop to help another, when we acknowledge that a hug is stronger than a slap, that those who exercise violence are cowards.

Sigmund Freud (1856-1939) coined the term "ego" in 1923 to enable him to further define psychological aspects of difference between the conscious state of mind and the unconscious state of mind. Freud's term entered the realm of western lexicon in the early twentieth century however Hindu thought preceded him by several thousand years. The construction of Vishnu temples is substantially influenced by symbolism of overt acknowledgement of Hindu belief. Nearest the ground, at the lowest level of the hierarchy of being are symbols depicting "abhiman" (Hindu for ego). The next level upward is "apsara" (nymphs or angels). Up, further still, are elephants, symbols of wisdom. Next higher, are horses that symbolize power, or better put, enablement. Interestingly enough, the uppermost symbols on the temple are from the Kama sutra. Fifty to sixty centuries prior to Dr. Freud, Hindu belief recognized the spiritual wellness of minimizing abhiman (ego) and maximizing love and affection.

"We need others. We need others to love and we need to be loved by them. There is no doubt that without it, we too, like the infant left alone, would cease to grow, cease to develop, choose madness and even death." – Dr. Leo Buscaglia (1924-1998). Dr. Buscaglia's quote, when coupled with the quote from Hermann Hesse at the beginning of this chapter, may provide an insight to the madness of the conflict in the Middle East and the other violent engagements throughout the planet. Just as a criminal mind/soul is warped to the point it cannot honor or recognize honesty and virtue, the violent mind/soul is so bereft of love it wallows in the quagmire of madness, hate, and terror. The Christian bible is remarkably accurate when it advises to "Love thine enemy" because only then will the emotional bankruptcy of the aggressor be exposed. Booker T. Washington was as eloquent as the passage from the bible when he remarked, "I will permit no man to narrow and degrade my soul by making me hate him." Should we opt to participate in the violence of the aggressor, we succeed only in lowering ourselves to their level or lower. That dynamic will never stop the cycle of pain and suffering of the innocents. To love is to express strength, to hate or harm is to express weakness.

The Christian bible and Islamic Qu'ran both contain inconsistencies as well as wisdom. One need not be a scholar or theologian to ask the following question but until those same scholars and/or theologians provide credible answers heeded by believers and/or laity, conflict in the Middle East may be perpetual. The first question to be posed is as follows, if Jesus Christ was the subject of an immaculate conception without the sexual consummation of either Joseph's sperm or Mary's egg, how could Jesus have been Jewish? If no flesh and blood link existed, no heritage between the mother and father of Jesus can be established. Jesus could not assume any aspect of their parentage because by definition, they were not his biological parents. If Mary or Joseph did not render egg and sperm, Mary's womb was merely an incubus. One may then ask, an incubus of what? Jesus, not being of them, has no claim to having Jewish lineage.

Beyond the alleged immaculate heritage of Christ, a conception without egg and sperm is not possible. In lay terms, if my wife came home and said, "Honey, I have just seen a gynecologist, you're not going to believe this… oh and it's the Son of God so we can't tell anybody, it's supposed to be a secret." With perspective this tale is not far-fetched it's completely fetched. Fiction becomes non-fiction when it is realized, i.e. made real.

Early neurotic detachment from sexual pleasure first arose from ancient Greece. Quoting from *The Reformation: A History* by Diarmaid MacCullough, "The Christian understanding of the roles of women and men in reproduction were also much influenced by the pre-Christian Aristotle, who presented the act of procreation as depending entirely on male seed. A man's semen contained the entire foetus in embryo: so anything which stopped male seed doing its job was an act of murder – anything, from masturbation to contraception to same-sex sexual relations. The idea was taken up by the second-century Christian teacher Clement of Alexandria, and it has become deeply imbedded in the Christian moral tradition, lying behind many of the pronouncements of the modern Roman Catholic Church on sexuality."[23] Mr. MacCulloch continues, "These assumptions in non-Christian authorities such as Galen were given further resonances by early Christian writers, particularly that towering authority Augustine of Hippo, who during his career as a theologian and bishop steadily developed a morbid horror of disorder, which was the product of fallen human self-will. He saw orgasm as the ultimate disorder, and tied it to the Christian myth about the disobedience of Adam and Eve in the Garden of Eden. ...The Church has been trying to tell private parts what to do ever since."[24] An adage came out of the Viet Nam war that was attributed to Lyndon Baines Johnson, "Get them by the balls and their hearts and minds will follow." President Johnson must have been at least somewhat familiar with the religio-political works of Saint Augustine.

Fundamental errors exist within the Qu'ran that also serve to confuse people who profess belief in the inspirational accuracy of the Qu'ran. Qu'ran verses 7:54, 10:4, and 11:7 tell of the creation of the heavens and earth in six days, Surah 7:54, "Lo! Your Lord is Allah Who created the heavens and earth in six Days, then mounted He the Throne. He covereth the night with the day, which is in haste to follow it, and hath made the sun and the moon and the stars subservient by His command. His verily is all creation and commandment. Blessed be Allah, the Lord of the Worlds. Yet we find a contradiction in Surah

41:9-12, " Say (O Muhammad, unto the idolators): Disbelieve ye verily in Him Who created the earth in two days, and ascribe ye unto Him rivals? He (and none else) is the Lord of the worlds. He placed therein firm hills rising above it, and blessed it and measured therein its sustenance in four Days, alike for (all) who ask. Then turned He to the heaven when it was smoke, and said unto it and unto the earth: Come both of you willingly or loathe. They said: We come obedient. Then He ordained them seven heavens in two Days and inspired in each heaven its mandate; and we decked the nether heaven with lamps, and rendered it inviolable. That is the measuring of the Mighty, the Knower." Creation of the earth, two days, firm hills and sustenance (topography, flora, and fauna) four days, and two days for the creation of the seven heavens clearly adds up to eight days.

The Qu'ran speaks of one paradise such as the paradise mentioned in verses 39:73, 41:30, 57:21 and 79:41. Yet other verses tell of many paradises, 18:32, 22:23, 35:33, 78:32, and 56:12. The Qu'ran provides contradictory verse on who gathers souls on Judgement Day. Surah 32:11 states, "Say: The angel of death, who hath charge concerning you, will gather you, and afterward unto your Lord ye will be returned." Yet Surah 39:42 renders another version of the final day, "Allah receiveth (men's) souls at the time of their death, and that (soul) which dieth not (yet) in its sleep. He keepeth that (soul) for which He hath ordained death and dismisseth the rest till an appointed term." No mention is made of the souls of women.

Contradiction exists regarding the creation of man. Surah 11:17 states that man was created from a clot of blood, Surahs 21:30 and 25:54 say man was created from water, Surahs 3:59 and 30:20 say dust, and Surah 15:26 says man was made from clay. Surah 2:62 says

Christians may enter heaven, "Lo! Those who believe (in that which is revealed unto thee, Muhammad), and those who are Jews, and Christians, and Sabaeans – whosoever believeth in Allah and the Last Day and doeth right - surely their reward is with their Lord, and there shall no fear come upon them neither shall they grieve." Yet, on the other hand, Surah 5:72, "They surely disbelieve who say: Lo! Allah is the Messiah, son of Mary. The Messiah (himself) said: O Children of Israel, worship Allah, my Lord and your Lord. Lo! Whoso ascribeth partners unto Allah, for him Allah hath forbidden Paradise. His abode is fire. For evil-doers there will be no helpers."

Discrepancies also lie in Islamic hadith, which are considered essential supplements to, and clarifications of, the Qu'ran. Citing a translation of Sahih Bukhari, volume 5, book 58, number 236, "Narrated Hisham's father: Khadia died three years before the Prophet departed to Medina. He stayed there for two years or so and then he married 'Aisha when she was a girl of six years of age, and then he consumated that marriage when she was nine years old." Yet, the Qu'ran, Surah 54 *Al-Qamr* (The Moon), was revealed to Muhammad nine years before Hijrah. This being the case, 'Aisha had not been born before this revelation but was a young girl. This would seem to indicate she was perhaps in her early to late teens. Muhammad is acknowledged to have had as many as eleven wives which is more than the four considered allowable by Islam. The second question, which begs an answer, is how could Muhammad, the Prophet, have consummated one of his eleven marriages with a girl who was allegedly 9 years old? Translations, and differing eras notwithstanding, paedophilia or sex with a minor is not now nor has it ever been acceptable moral behavior The Qu'ran (or Recitation) was intended to be exactly that: a recited text. The establishment of Islamic canonical text is attributed to the third Caliph, Uthman, who appointed a committee headed by Zaid ibn Thabit, one of the scribes of the Prophet. The task of the committee was to gather evidence of revelations as revealed to Muhammad whether written on parchments, leaves, or stones, or by relying on memories of those who witnessed and memorized the words of the Prophet. This committee was formed twenty years after the death of Muhammad.

Hadith and the Qu'ran contain misinterpretations and error, as do the Old and New Testaments of the bible. If as Christian fundamentalists allege, Adam and Eve bore two sons, Cain and Abel, the further procreation of humanity would have been incestuous. The Christian Bible was not finalized until the Synod of Hippo in 393 A.D. This was approximately 350 years after the death of Christ. The doctrine that Jesus had been God in human form was not finalized until then. Furthermore, Jesus never claimed to be God. The earliest Gospels to be included in the New Testament at the behest of Irenaeus were written 40-60 years after Christ's death. These texts must have contained elements of error, bias, and motive. This dynamic of error must exist too regarding the recording, and transcription of the prophesies of Mohammed that became Islamic scripture. Canonization of the Bible and Qu'ran were done centuries if not decades after the fact and in both cases are immanently subject to error and misinterpretation.

Interpretation or fantastic lore is not limited to Christianity and Islam. Judaism has its share as well. A midrash is a method of exegesis of Biblical text. In the same way that hadith supplement and clarify Islam, midrashim aim to supplement the Tanakh (Jewish Bible) with exegetical or homiletical commentaries. Two such midrashim about the presentation of the Torah at Mount Sinai read as follows:

"The Lord came unto Sinai; after having [first] risen at Seir unto the people thereof. Then having shined forth at Mount Paran, He came unto the myriads holy. At His right hand a fiery law for them" (deut. 33:2). When he who is everywhere revealed Himself to give the Torah to Israel, He revealed Himself not only to Israel, but to all other nations as well. At first, God went to the children of Esau. He asked them: Will you accept the Torah? They said right to His face: What is written in it? He said: "Thou shalt not murder." They replied: "Master of the universe, this goes against our grain. Our father, whose "hands are the hands of Esau" (Gen. 27:22), led us to rely only on the sword, because his father told him, "By thy sword shalt thou live" (Gen. 27:40). We cannot accept the Torah. Then He went to the children of Ammon and Moab and asked them: Will you accept the Torah? They said right to His face, "What is written in it?" He said, "Thou shalt not commit adultery." They replied: Master of the universe, our very origin is in adultery, for Scripture says, "Thus were both the daughters of Lot with child by their father (Gen. 27:40). We cannot accept the Torah. Then He went to the children of Ishmael. He asked them: Will you accept the Torah? They said right to his face: What is written in it? He said: "Thou shalt not steal." They replied: Master of the universe, it is our very nature to live off only what is stolen and what is got by assault. Of our forbear Ishmael it is written, "And he shall be a wild ass of a man: his hand shall be against every man, and every man's hand against him" (Gen. 16:12). We cannot accept the Torah. There was not a single nation among the nations to whom God did not go, speak, and, as it were, knock on its door, asking whether it would be willing to accept the

Torah. At long last, He came to Israel. They said, "We will do and hearken" (Exodus 24:7). Of God's successive attempts to give the Torah, it is written, "the Lord came unto Sinai; after having [first] risen at Seir unto the people thereof, then having shined forth at Mount Paran, He finally came unto the myriads holy, at His right hand a fiery law for them" (Deut. 33:2).

A second midrash, this one by Rabbi Avdimi bar Hama is at least 1500 years old and can be found in the Babylonian Talmud, Shabbat p. 88a, 32, "And they stood under the mount" (Exodus 19:17). R. Avdimi bar Hama said: The verse implies that the Holy One overturned the mountain upon them, like an inverted cask, and said to them: If you accept the Torah, it is well; if not, your grave will be right here." Why would God have to threaten anyone to accept divine law? Why when offered, would anyone decline God's law? Further still, how can a people consider themselves as God's chosen people if the law had to be rendered unto them under threat of annihilation?

Strange indeed that there seem to be so many parallels in these religions which ironically, work at cross-purposes attempting to accomplish the same thing, i.e. the salvation of souls. Odd it is that each religion tries to assume credit for that which is the eternal birthright of Homo Divinitas, the gift of eternal life.

As mentioned in *A New Reformation*, the three books of faith, Talmud, Qu'ran, and Bible have much in common. Quoting from *The Age of Faith* by Will Durant, "Some of these elements in creed and practice may have been a common heritage of the Semites; some of them – angels, devils, Satan, heaven, hell, the resurrection, the Last Judgment – had been taken by the Jews from Babylonia or Persia, and may have gone directly from Persia to Islam. In Zoroastrian, as in Mohammedan, eschatology, the resurrected dead must walk upon a perilous bridge over a deep abyss; the wicked fall into hell, the good pass into a paradise where they enjoy, among other dainties, the society of women (houris) whose beauty and ardor will last forever. To Jewish theology, ethics, and ritual, and Persian eschatology, Mohammed added Arab demonology, pilgrimage, and the Kaaba ceremony, and made Islam."[25]

"The three religions agreed in rejecting the practicability of a natural-non-religious-mortality; most men, they believed, can be persuaded to tolerable behavior only by the fear of God. All three based their moral code on identical conceptions: the all-seeing eye and all-recording hand of God, the divine authorship of the moral code, and the ultimate equalization of virtue with happiness by post-mortem punishments and rewards. In the two Semitic cultures law, as well as ethics, was inseparable from religion; no distinction was admitted between crime and sin, between civil and ecclesiastical law; every discreditable act is an offense against God, a profanation of His presence and holy Name."[26]

"Three books made and almost filled the Age of Faith: the Bible, the Talmud, the Koran – as if to say that in the rebarbarization of the Roman Empire only a supernatural ethic could restore society order to society and the soul. All three books were Semitic, and overwhelmingly Judaic. The drama of medieval history would be the spiritual competition of these scriptures and the bloody conflict of their creeds."[27] The power of religious thought has not accented the similarities within we/they it has exacerbated the differences. Salvation, as opposed to reincarnation, mandates church membership *now*. Recruitment and dues are necessary adjuncts to membership. On the face of it, does it not seem ludicrous, in all of timeless eternity, to have one and only one shot at the golden ring? But certain religions would have you *believe* so. Control of the mind is ever so subtle yet ever so powerful. Youngsters who have been exposed, indoctrinated, programmed, or brainwashed with any system of thought have not had the opportunity of choice to exercise free will. Tragically that legacy could continue for a lifetime.

Inconsistencies and conflict exist in the arena of governmental politics when the United States presumes to export democracy on a ready or not basis. In so doing, the U.S. becomes not as former United States Secretary of State Colin Powell would say, the "good cop" it becomes a bully. The administration of the U.S. government displays hypocrisy vis-à-vis its stated goal, be it Manifest Destiny at the beginning of the 20th Century (the Panama Canal) or making the world safe for democracy at the beginning of the 21st century (Iraq) when it consistently favors business interests rather than the wishes of the people it presumes to champion. Nothing has changed in 100 years.

Recently Keith Olbermann of MSNBC News offered this prescient quote from Rod Serling, "The tools of conquest do not necessarily come with bombs and explosions and fallout. They are weapons that are simply thoughts, attitudes, prejudices, to be found only in the minds of men." Prejudice and hypocrisy are evident when the U.S. fails to respect the freely elected governments in Venezuela, Chile (under Allende), Hezbullah, or the Palestinian Liberation Organization. Hypocrisy is further evident when the United States government supports corrupt and/or immoral regimes such as those of Ferdinand Marcos in the Phillipines or Shah Reza Pahlavi in Iran that contradict the principles of republican government or democracy in lieu of corruption and/or favor. Hypocrisy is apparent when George W. Bush willfully ignores the situation in Myanmar where brutal thugs of a military junta enslave the populace. His hypocrisy is further apparent when he ignores the country of Nepal whose people have valiantly struggled against Maoist rebels and an ineffective and corrupt monarchy. And still further when he remains mute in the face of the repression of the people of Zimbabwe by the brutal Robert Mugabe. And yet again, when it fails to sponsor and encourage a seat for the most populous democracy on earth, India, to have a seat on the United Nations Security Council.

If Mr. Bush were authentic in his conviction to further democracy (or better still, elective government of *their* own choosing) on the world stage, U.S. foreign policy would assist *all* who wish to be free, not just those who provide oil. I have no doubt Mr. Bush is sincere in his efforts, but then too, used car dealers are sincere. There is more to elected government than the vote. A free society requires, among other requisites, a free and open communication media, an independent judiciary, and uncompromising law enforcement and the capacity to develop municipal and rural infrastructures. When such elements of society are in place, the elective process has veracity and thus the full force of mandate of the electorate can enforce elective choices. The debacle in Iraq has borne this out.

Ironically, the United States was formed as a republic and was intended to remain so. Aristotle said that "republics decline into democracies and democracies degenerate into despotisms." If Mr. Bush wanted to emulate the founding fathers of the United States, he would endeavor to expound upon *republican* form of government as opposed to a democracy. Centuries of political assault on the

---

[i] "Nothing is more unpredictable than the mob, nothing more obscure than public opinion, nothing more deceptive than the whole political system."

constitution have morphed the government of the United States into a 51% government. "A democracy is nothing more than mob rule where 51% of the people may take away the rights of the other 49%. – Thomas Jefferson. Nihil est incertius vulgo, nihil obscurius voluntate hominum, nihil fallacius ratione tota comitiorum.ⁱ– Cicero (106 B.C. – 43 B.C.). Democracy is a form of government that permits two drunks to outvote a genius thus explaining why politics consists of a cesspool of participants who appeal to "inebriants" for their votes.

The juxtaposition of views between Aristotle and George W. Bush reminds this author of a televised 1988 vice-presidential debate between the patrician patriarch of Texas politics Lloyd Bentson and Dan Quayle of Indiana. Quayle noted that he had as much political experience as John F. Kennedy when Kennedy ran for office. Bentsen fired back with the retort "Senator, I served with Jack Kennedy. I knew Jack Kennedy. Jack Kennedy was a friend of mine. Senator, you're no Jack Kennedy". Dubya, you're no Aristotle.

Politics and politicians cast a pall on death in the same way a pall is cast on the affairs of Homo Divinitas. United States governmental protocol requires flags to be lowered to half-staff upon the death of a president to signify mourning of his passing. Gerald Ford is the most recent president to be so honored. Mr. Ford died of natural cause at age 93. Conversely, a soldier who dies in combat following orders from the commander-in-chief while defending his or her country does not have the flag lowered to commemorate the honor of his or her ultimate sacrifice. Upon the death of George W. Bush, he too will have the flag lowered to acknowledge mourning of the death of a president. Tragically, thousands of men and women in uniform who have lost their lives with no choice other than to follow

Mr. Bush's policies will suffer a silent epitaph. Old Glory will never be lowered to honor them when they are lowered into the ground from whence they came.

Politicians know fully well that market studies and demographic indicators tell them to market their pitch to the gullible, naïve or uneducated because they far outnumber geniuses in market share. This is why, perhaps as a last resort, the founding fathers of the American Republic instituted the Electoral College to elect the president, precisely to prevent mob-rule. States of the union elect presidents, people do not, *nor were they intended to.* "It could probably be shown by facts and figures that there is no native criminal class except congress." – Mark Twain (1835-1910). Nothing has changed in 100 years. "Dubya" as a professing Christian in particular, and politicians from all continents should heed Carlyle, "Make yourself an honest man, and then you may be sure there is one less rascal in the world."

In the arena of religious politics, when Muslims kill in the name of Allah, they are no more than bullies in the religious arena. "War is an instrument entirely inefficient toward redressing wrong; and multiplies, instead of indemnifying losses." – Thomas Jefferson. Yet, just as democracies or despots maneuver for power without regard for political sovereignty of a foreign nation, religions proselytize just as avidly to bring salvation to the masses. Religious recruiters (proselytizers) or combatants (jihadists) are not bound by and consequently do not honor borders. Nor, for the most part, do they respect the spiritual sovereignty of a potential convert (target).

Personal sovereignty is the sanctity of one's own body and soul, not that of someone else. My compact with the Great Integrity is one-to-one and requires only the influences **I** deem necessary. If we love ourselves more fully, it becomes easier to love, or at minimum, tolerate thine enemy, if only for the reason that if we hate our enemy, we become haters, and thus become those whom we profess to hate. Love is the answer. Love takes courage, love takes understanding, love entails sacrifice. A mountaintop cannot be reached without pain; yet the mountaintop does not beckon the coward, it calls out to the poet, to the courageous, and to those who know the truest strength belongs not in the fingers of a fist so much as in the arms of a caress.

If we cannot extend the aegis of love the least we can attempt is tolerance of each other and understanding of each other. For that we need look no farther than the Qu'ran. Surah 109 was revealed to the Prophet (Mohammad) when idolaters asked him to compromise in matters of religion:

In the name of Allah, the Beneficent, the Merciful.

1. Say: O disbelievers!
2. I worship not that which ye worship.
3. Nor worship ye that which I worship.
4. And I shall not worship that which ye worship.
5. Nor will ye worship that which I worship.
6. Unto you your religion, and unto me my religion.

One can merely conjecture as to why such animosity exists between Sunni and Shia, between Muslim and Christian. Surely, prayers for peace will remain unanswered until we demonstrate the wisdom to hear and understand answers to those prayers. The answer for peace is quite simply to stop fighting and, if not love each other, at least learn and practice tolerance, insofar as to suppose that someone else may have a better answer. Those who profess Christianity above all else should do so after reading the "gospel" of all else. The Muslim who professes Islam above all else should do so having studied the "gospel" of all else. We should endeavor to share our likenesses instead of exploiting our differences. Experience dictates that politicians in both government and religion exacerbate differences in seeking leverage to climb the ever-enticing rungs of the ladders of electoral or nominative power. And make no mistake; the political animal would rather climb to power amid conflict than be powerless in peace.

Politicians who refer to the occupation of high political office as service to country should reconsider the context of their perspective. Service to one's country, such as it is, is typified by the nurse in the M.A.S.H. unit giving care and understanding to a wounded soldier. Service to one's country may be volunteering in the Peace Corps and with blood, sweat, and tears, helping to improve the quality of life of families other than their own. The concept of service is predicated on the premise that the one who provides care and service does not benefit more than those to whom the service is intended. Disservice to one's country is when officials seek and obtain elective office using millions of dollars of other people's money to make a six-figure salary, and in so doing, enjoy and subsequently corrupt the perks of prestige, privilege, and power. Service is caring for others without asking for or receiving equitable compensation. Elected officials who sate their own gluttony on the bounty of the public trough are not serving but self-serving.

In spite of political apparatchiks who create inter-border and inter-faith animosity by exploiting differences in order to justify their participation in, and exercise of faux-power, Homo Divinitas desires unrestricted worship of the Creator and freedom to experience the spectacular miracle of life. This can be done in so many ways, so many languages. It matters not that we sing in one voice, or with words of one verse, it matters only that we sing our worship fully and with all our hearts. This book is not about salvation or damnation because, at least to the author, those concepts are not plausible. That said, the politicians of government and religion who sow and reap the harvest of seeds of polarization, fear, and force, would be the truest candidates for damnation. Ultimately what this author does find plausible, is not to blame them for depravity though they are fully aware of their actions and ramifications thereof, but prove to them there is a better way; the way of atonement and subsequent forgiveness.

Changing one's heart from kindness to vengeance is an act of weakness and must be recognized as such. Changing the vengeful heart to one of forgiveness is divine. If mankind does not exercise the strength to understand and forgive, we serve merely to perpetuate and/or exacerbate the present condition of man, our spiritus mundi. Bigotry, exploitation, fear, and terror, are weapons of the weak of mind and weak of character. May we concentrate less on *we/they* and more on *we*. May we concentrate on our similarities rather than exploit our differences. Hate is the deepest expression of emotional impotence. Forgiveness, tolerance, love, all require courage. Love is the deepest expression of affection tempered by the strength of fidelity and honor. It is said that a dog would be so loving and innocent as to lick the hand of its killer. In such a way, I seek to emulate the wholesomeness of the pet and infuse my life with happiness as opposed to the despair of the violence of the ignorant.

CHAPTER 7
THE NATURE OF POLITICS

"Good intentions will always be pleaded for every assumption of authority. It is hardly too strong to say that the constitution was made to guard the people against the dangers of good intentions. There are men in all ages who mean to govern well, but they mean to govern. They promise to be good masters, but they mean to be masters."
– Daniel Webster (1782-1852).

Any society that would give up a little liberty to gain a little security will deserve neither and lose both.
– Benjamin Franklin (1706-1790).

One need not possess the prodigious intellect and wisdom of Mr. Franklin or Mr. Webster to assume the mantle of greatness in the arena of governance. In lieu of possession of such intellect and wisdom, one must have the emotional and intellectual gravitas to realize wisdom for what it is and adopt it as such. George ("Dubya") Bush's failures are due to the fact he seemingly possesses virtually no wisdom of his own and is reliant (almost in the Romanov sense) on the political instincts of his own Rasputin (Karl Rove). "Dubya" has not the inclination or desire to recognize or assimilate the wisdom of great minds that preceded him. Political carnivores that force or enforce government through usurpation of power do so with a direct correlation to the lessening of power and freedom of the governed. When requesting congress to draft the Patriot Act, "Dubya" was not aware of, or chose to disregard the wisdom of Benjamin Franklin. "Dubya" also was not aware of or chose to disregard Thomas Paine (1737-1809) who said, "He that would make his own liberty secure, must guard even his enemy from opposition. For if he violates this duty, he establishes a precedent that will reach himself."

This is not to say that politicians in general and "Dubya" in particular do not possess empathy or compassion. Esquire Magazine dutifully reported in their February 2007 issue of "Dubya's" evident compassion when visiting wounded veterans in Texas in 2006, "President Bush offered consolation to wounded veterans at the Amputee Care Center of Brooke Army Medical Center in San Antonio by saying, "I have an injury myself – not here at the hospital, but in combat with a cedar. I eventually won. The cedar gave me a little scratch." Having not heard this remark to understand any verbal context in which it was made, the remark is either remarkably callous and detached or in remarkably poor taste. History has confirmed the veracity and wisdom of Messrs. Franklin and Paine. History will remember "Dubya" far less favorably.

Power corrupts and absolute power corrupts absolutely. Power uses leverage, manipulation, and patronage to exercise hegemony and power begins with money. Constituent representation is obfuscated when supra-constituent monetary contributions tilt the scale of financial advantage in favor of a candidate. The will of the people is accurately expressed in elective government solely if and when the wishes of any constituency are executed without contamination by outside influence or favor. Political ideology thrives on influence however influence can be bought, especially with the tool of supra-constituent campaign money. After all, governments are filled with prostitutes; the sole difference among them is the amount on their price tag.

Public policy results from the "physics" of two colliding forces. One such force is the dedication to ideology or in rare instance, principle or conscience. Contamination of law by graft and expedience is the other opposing force. Legislation is bastardized when the illegitimacy of corruption compels lawmakers weak of principle or conscience to act on behalf of the interests of lobbyists (pimps) who finance incumbency as opposed to the common good of the commonweal i.e. their constituencies. Legislation is flawed in direct proportion to the factor of corruption that enters the equation of political discourse. Again quoting Thomas Paine, "A thing moderately good is not as good as it ought to be. Moderation in temper is always a virtue; but moderation in principle is always a vice." Politics is the midwife of bastard legislation.

Lord Edward Cecil (1867-1918) defined compromise (as), "An agreement between two men to do what both agree is wrong." Quoting the English writer G.K. Chesterton, "Compromise used to mean that half a loaf was better than no bread. Among modern statesmen it really seems to mean that a half a loaf is better than a whole loaf." Mr. Chesterton died in 1936. It would seem that seventy years hence, the politicians end up with the entire loaf baked by the ever-rising yeast of taxation. Janis Joplin was a rock star, not a person of letters, yet she was more eloquent than any politician when she said, "Don't compromise yourself, you are all you've got."

History has recorded the barbarity of conquerors from Attila to Hitler, from the debauchery of the Caesars, to the brutality of Idi Amin Dada (Uganda) and the regime of Pol Pot (Cambodia) and al-Bashir of Sudan. There is however, a more subtle type of tyranny than that of the conqueror; it is that of the common ideologue. Ideologues have the same motive and purpose as the conqueror, however the dimension of time serves to blur the perception of their pursuit of rule. A conqueror seeks immediate reign, while an ideologue has enough patience and finesse to wait. Tyranny and despotism seek power in much the same way a spider captures its prey, one thread at a time. Ideologies, which are generally couched in terms of we/they seek domination whether by the politics of governance or religion. Politicians exploit differences for personal aggrandizement.

In 1966 Robert Wise directed the film *The Sand Pebbles* based on the novel written by Richard McKenna and the screenplay of Robert Anderson. Steve McQueen stars in the film as engineer Jake Holman. Holman essentially had no home as a child and was given the choice of army, navy, or reform school after punching his high school principal. Sir Richard Attenborough starred as Frenchy Burgoyne, Candice Bergen as a teacher named Shirley Eckert who is based at the mission, (who falls in love with Holman), Richard Crenna as Captain Collins, and Larry Gates as Mr. Jameson, the head of the mission. The U.S.S. San Pablo represents the interests of the United States in revolution-torn China of 1926. Captain Collins is a quintessential patriotic duty-driven gunboat commander. Jake Holman is an iconoclast with strains of cynicism laced with idealism. Against the backdrop of ever escalating conflict, the San Pablo crashes through a protective river-boom to rescue missionaries upriver at the China Light Mission. The dialog of the scene begins as Captain Collins and his landing party enter the mission (at grave risk) to affect the rescue. Missionary Jameson sees the approaching party and,

Jameson: "Lieutenant Collins, it would be much better for all of us if you'd go away at once. We have no intention of leaving."

Collins: "Your lives are in danger."

Jameson: "You shouldn't have come here."

Collins: "Jameson, you're to come back with me. You have five minutes to pack whatever you need."

Jameson: "Our militia of students went to fight you at the boom. I was hoping to see them come back victorious instead of you."

Collins: "You heard about Nanking?"

Jameson: "Yes. Those events have no bearing here. You alone endanger us. I must ask you to leave now."

Collins: "My duty is to protect you."

Jameson: "No longer. Shirley, will you please get that paper from my desk. (Then to Collins) We've declared ourselves stateless persons. We've sent our names to Geneva."

Collins: "That's impossible!"

Jameson: "Read this.

(While Collins is reading, an aside by Eckert to Holman), Eckert: "Jake."

Holman (looking at Eckert): I tried to get back sooner but I couldn't make it. Are you staying?"

Eckert: Yes. What happened at the boom?"

Seeing that Collins has now finished reading the declaration, Jameson: "By that signed declaration, we have renounced nationality itself. Your uniform now gives you no authority over us and no responsibility for us."

Collins: "This is romantic nonsense!"

Jameson: "We convinced most of the people here that there is no connection whatsoever between ourselves and the gunboats. Your presence only endangers us."

Collins: "You are warned Jameson. They'll kill you."

Jameson: "They will not."

Collins: Perhaps once, this might have protected you but not now. Now it is shooting and killing. It's too late for such fine distinctions."

Jameson: "It will protect us."

Collins: "This afternoon, my ship fought its way through, down there at the boom. People were killed on both sides. You are not going to make that a futile and meaningless battle."

Jameson: "We will not serve to give meaning to your heroics. Our lives have their own meaning. We have renounced nationality."

Collins: "You have been sentenced to death by their courts."

Jameson: "I am free under the protection of one of their students who is their leader."

Collins: "They do not care who protects you now, not after Nanking. And it will not be a student militia who comes for you now but regular troops. Miss Eckert, they will strip you and rape you. And then this whole valley will be destroyed when our country comes to avenge your death. Do you want that?"

Eckert: "You don't know them."

Jameson: "When have you ever cared for Chinese women raped and butchered by the warlord troops you favor with your unequal treaties? In heavens name, leave us alone."

Collins: "That's enough. Holman, help them get their things together."

Holman: "No sir."

Jameson: "That's an order."

Holman: "You'd better get back to the ship captain, 'cause they're stayin' here and so am I."

Jameson: "D'you know what this is? Desertion in the face of the enemy."

Holman: "I ain't got no more enemies…shove off captain."

At this point the scene is such that a wounded Chinese man staggers into the courtyard, staggers into Jameson's arms and struggles to tell him of impending attack upon the monastery.

Jameson: "Shirley, he says Cho-Jen is dead."

Eckert: "Oh No, No."

Jameson (Staring at Collins with the frustration of rage and sorrow welling up into tears he cries): "You killed him at the boom and now they're coming for me. Because of you and your blind pride. DAMN YOUR FLAG (sobbing in grief). DAMN ALL FLAGS. It's too late in this world for flags." Gunshots begin to be fired throughout the courtyard and minutes later Jameson is fatally wounded.

The final scene of the movie is when Holman, alone in the dark courtyard is providing cover for shipmates who are trying to take Shirley Eckert back to the San Pablo. Holman has just been seriously wounded and realizes his last moments may be at hand. In one last attempt, he raises his rifle, and while doing so, says to himself, "I was home. What happened? **What the hell happened**?" The next moment he is fatally shot. Those last words of the movie are his epitaph, **and our own if we do not change our mindset of existence**. His *home* was with his love, Shirley, in a mission that did not recognize borders. He *realized* he had no enemies when he made the emotional choice to remain with her and not return to the ship. At that moment, he realized he had no enemies. The *home* of Homo Divinitas ultimately exists without flags, without borders, and with the ones we love. When we make those choices, when we realize (make real) the elimination of borders, enemies will cease to be real. Reality has the gravitas we render to it. Reality is created by effort applied to thought. We can de-create borders and flags when we so choose to realize de-creation of imaginary political borders.

Regarding territorial borders, an interesting parallel exists with the scriptural (both Bible and Qu'ran) definition of usury. The parallel comparison of territorial borders with usury follows that, just as time and hope dwell wholly within the province of God's creation, so does the land of God's creation on which we live. Territorial borders are occult political conjurations that are superimposed upon and thus cause the imaginary partition of the planet Earth. Political borders determine geographical boundaries of power and rule for a nation-state. Within a nation-state, title to land demarcates boundary of ownership for the private individual. By creating ownership, such political and legal borders establish and determine, a priori, land *value*. Thus, ownership of, or claim to land, ipso facto, creates both political and occult financial value by preventing use and/or occupation of land by those who wish or mean to do so. Those with intent to occupy land may do so only through purchase (subject to usury) or conquest. In this lose/lose scenario, either choice is demeaning. By contrast, aboriginal peoples who are more in touch with spirituality believe *they belong to the land, they do not own land.*

Seemingly, scriptures seem to indicate that man has no right to profit from God's time or God's land…unless it's for the fiduciary benefit of the church. Quoting Carmen Rene Berry's The Unauthorized Guide to Sex and the Church, "At the core of property rights is the issue of who controls whom and who controls what. The institutionalized church was driven by the desire to expand its control over people and to amass as much wealth and land as possible. This desire may have been shrouded in theological language, but the behavior of popes, councils, and others in leadership reveals their true motives. Women were seen as competitors with the church for the loyalty of their husbands, especially those men who served as clergy. The church did not like the fact that inheritance rights traditionally passed on a family's holdings to children. Instead, it wanted everyone who joined the clergy, convent or monastery to make the church the recipient of their inherited wealth. At times in history, priests were allowed to couple with women – to live with them, have sex with them, and have children – as long as the women were not given the status of "wife" and the children were not acknowledged as heirs."[28] Further quoting Ms. Berry regarding property rights and the Catholic Church, "In an overt effort to bring land and wealth under the church's domain, Pope Innocent II and the Second Lateran Council seized land assets of married priests and demoted their wives to the status of concubines."[29] This medieval attitude toward property was not left behind in the Middle Ages. "When the missionaries came to Africa they had the Bible and we had the land. They said, "Let us pray." We closed our eyes. When we opened them we had the Bible and they had the land." – Bishop **Desmond Tutu**. Bishop Tutu has won the Albert Schweitzer Prize for Humanitarianism, the Gandhi Peace Prize, and the Alfred Nobel Peace Prize. One is not surprised by candor from such a person as this.

A case can be made that assigning occult financial value to the land of God's creation is as morally indefensible as assigning occult financial value, i.e. interest, i.e. usury to the dimension of time and the element of hope, both of which are part of God's creation. Further still, regarding the planet on which we live, it is just as fallacious to assign occult political identity with, and fealty to, a nation-state. In an imperfect world, upon the moment of birth, every child is involuntarily and indelibly stamped with political identity, a political obligation as it were, to a nation-state, a *nationality*. Alluding to the previous quote from Buddhism, east and west are random distinctions of man as well as the borders that determine Ohio and Indiana, France and Germany. Just as the early church entered an unholy poltical power-sharing détente with Roman government, it remains ineffective when it continues to polticize worship and the misdeeds of its clergy.

Nations legislate juris law. Juris law determines jurisdiction and jurisdiction determines parameters of lawful behavior and accountability to those laws. Jurisdiction of Right of Abode is primarily determined *jus soli* (by right of territory) or *jus sanguinas* (by right of blood[line]). Politics of law determines the occult political status or persona of man, i.e. citizen, alien, or refugee, vis-à-vis his or her relation to other nations. "Nationality" when predicated on arbitrary circumstance of the geography of one's birth, limits identity with, and access to our fellow human family. Someone's nationality, which is to say, their occult political identity, presupposes differences in the human family of man, when in fact we all have essentially the same needs and wants. Nationalities serve to obfuscate our similarities and exacerbate our differences. Yes, naturalization processes do exist whereby a person may change nationality yet the fundamental fallacy is to accept the occult circumstance that we must have a political affiliation at all or that it must be subject to governmental process and approval. The Scarlet Letter of Nationality stamped on our foreheads is contrary to the concept of Homo Divinitas as one family with, and of, God, Allah, the Great Integrity.

In a perfect world, consider Homo Divinitas as he and she were meant to be. Ideally, Homo Divinitas should exist in a world whereby he or she, as Divinity's creation, may elect to exercise the Right of Abode as a divine mandate to live anywhere on Divinity's creation without regard to occult political restrictions (borders) that serve to divide the human family, thereby eschewing any political identity over which they initially had no choice. This Universal Right of Abode would be determined *jus divinitas genesis.* Homo Divinitas is of divine creation and thus, should have unfettered access to the planet of his birthright and the brethren of the family thereon, a child of Divinity's creation with unlimited access to Divinity's creation…a stateless person in a stateless (not to be confused with lawless) world.

"National hatred is strongest and most vehement on the lowest stage of culture. But there is a stage where it totally disappears and where one stands, so to say, above the nations and feels the good fortune or distress of his neighbor people as if it happened to his own." – German philosopher Johann Wolfgang von Goethe (1749-1832). Philosophers the world over have determined that hatred is directly proportionate to ignorance just as there seems to be a direct correlation between forgiveness and wisdom. "A loving heart is the beginning of all knowledge". – Thomas Carlysle.

The need for lawmakers is minimized and the influence of politicians is eliminated when political borders are eliminated (de-realized). Those who make law and enforce order would still be necessary, however the freedom to live anywhere, the Right of Universal Abode, without the restraint of occult political borders would compel lawmakers and law enforcement to serve the immediate interest of the commonweal and the inertia of brotherhood instead of isolation and the perpetual conflict of we/they. Reassuming and realizing the

Right of Universal Abode enables Homo Divinitas to express the freedom to transverse borders of oppression such as those in North Korea, Myanmar, Afghanistan, China, Sudan, and Zimbabwe. The power of despotism is neutered and the free flow of physical freedom leads to and is congruent with spiritual and bodily freedom.

Flags are political banners that reinforce imaginary lines drawn on dirt. Flags create animosity between nations thus creating a need for political solutions for politically created problems! Augustine's doctrine of "original sin" institutionalized a need for salvation, hence the power of the church! Politicians exacerbate and exploit differences to justify their presence rather than focusing on similarities which could lead to brotherhood of the human family. Homo Divinitas has the divine right to physical sovereignty just as he has a divine entitlement to spiritual sovereignty. Now is the time to proceed to and fully participate in the freedoms of full physical and spiritual emancipation.

Military armament of any country is merely a potential arm of enforcement for ideologues of government. Ideologies lacking moral content require force for perpetuation. Dueling with pistols merely determines who is quickest on the draw, who has least patience, or whose egos are most insecure. Dueling, i.e. force, does not have the intellectual veracity of open debate of the stage of ideas. Weak doctrine will beg pistols and bombs. Wholesome doctrine needs no reinforcement. Ideologues in the quest of power presume to usurp moral grounds to bolster their claims of faux righteousness. Daniel Webster's words are as prescient today as they were more than one hundred years ago.

The nest in which ideology is born, incubated, and nurtured is that of the political party. In the manner of the political party, the torch (party slate) remains the same though the individual who bears the torch may change. In any race, distance is covered by a single runner (ideologue) or a relay team (ideology). What matters after all, is winning, i.e. the implementation and continuity of ideology and therefore incumbency. If this were not the case, politicians would have a code of conduct such as those established for boxing by the Marquis of Queensbury. This not being the case, the only rule is (Parliamentary Procedure notwithstanding) that it is appropriate to try to get away with breaking all the rules to further the interests of the party. Politicians have not learned that ends do not justify the means, or if they have, they elect to disregard means and end in lieu of the aphrodisiac of power.

As Adolph Hitler rose to power in Germany of the 1930's, his deputy, Rudolf Hess, quite often introduced him to the adoring crowd. Hess would build the intensity of the crowd with anticipation for the Fuhrer with statements such as, "Die partei ist Hitler, und Hitler ist die partei." Such is the dynamic of the perpetuation of ideology through political parties(ei's).

Parties continually walk a fine line between responding to their constituents and battling for the power and influence of incumbency in a two-party system of electoral government. Political lobbies serve to exert national pressure on local constituencies. National lobbies such as the NRA, AIPAC (Israeli interests), Pharmaceuticals, Oil, etc, contaminate politics by trumping local matters with national influence and financial leverage. No party will be so self-effacing as to put the welfare of the local electorate ahead of their own national agenda. No lobby will be so self-effacing as to respect the wishes of the local constituency over their own selfish agenda.

Partisan (is there any other kind?) party politics prohibits the "outs" from helping the "ins" because a country that is functioning well will reelect "ins" at the expense of "outs". Consequently "outs" have no reason to assist "ins" because to do so would perpetuate incumbency of the "ins" and would only serve in gutting their own power-lust. "There is no reason to accept the doctrines crafted to sustain power and privilege, or to believe that we are constrained by mysterious and unknown social laws. These are simply decisions made within institutions that are subject to human will and that must face the test of legitimacy. And if they do not meet the test, they can be replaced by other institutions that are more free and more just, as has happened often in the past." – Noam Chomsky. Grover Norquist, a powerful neoconservative strategist was, if nothing else, candid when he remarked, "Bipartisanship is another form of date rape." Though no democrat has yet been quoted to that effect, it is reasonable to surmise that the same opinion is held on both sides of the aisle. Democratic party pit-bull James Carville expressed a somewhat different though no less intriguing viewpoint when he said, "The Democratic constituency is just like a herd of cows. All you have to do is lay out enough silage and they come running. That's why I became an operative working with Democrats. With Democrats all you have to do is make a lot of noise, lay out the hay, and be ready to use the ole cattle prod in case a few want to bolt the herd." In this way, there is little if any difference between democrat, republican, conservative, liberal, or Baathist.

We cannot presume to believe that politicians have the interest of the electorate at heart. We can merely presume to accept that occasionally we may benefit, however only as a by-product of the collateral damage resulting from the collision of partisan political antitheses. Statesmen are bound by conscience and loyalty to the welfare of their state. Politicians have no comprehension of the term "loyalty" and are steadfastly bound and exercise fealty only to the party(ei).

Partisanship has been most blatantly expressed in the congressional elections of 2006. Excerpting a commentary from Keith Olbermann (MSNBC) that first aired on November 2, 2006, " On the 22nd of May, 1856, as the deteriorating American political system veered toward the edge of the cliff, U.S. Representative Preston Brooks of South Carolina shuffled into the senate of this nation, his leg stiff from an old dueling injury, supported by a cane. And he looked for the familiar figure of the prominent senator from Massachusetts, Charles Sumner. Brooks found Sumner at his desk, mailing out copies of a speech he had delivered three days earlier – a speech against slavery. The congressman matter-of-factly raised his walking stick in midair and smashed its metal point across the senator's head. Congressman Brooks hit his victim repeatedly. Senator Sumner somehow got to his feet and tried to flee. Brooks chased him and delivered untold blows to Sumner's head. Even though Sumner lay unconscious and bleeding on the Senate floor, Brooks finally stopped beating him only because his cane finally broke. Others will cite John Brown's attack on the arsenal at Harper's ferry as the exact point after which the Civil War became inevitable. In point of fact, it might have been the moment, not when Brooks broke his cane over the prostrate body of senator Sumner – but when voters in Brooks' district started sending him new canes." Continuing, "There is tonight no political division in this country that he (Bush) and his party will not exploit, nor have not exploited; no anxiety that he and his party will not inflame." Mr. Olbermann then recounts the botched joke by Senator John Kerry (D-Mass.). When Sen. Kerry speaking of the tragically inept and misdirected war in Iraq, remarked that, "if you make the most of it, you study hard, you do your homework, and you make an effort to be smart, you can do well. If you don't, you'll get struck in Iraq." Speaking of the partisan political response to the joke, Mr. Olbermann continues, "He (John McCain (R-Az.) rolled over and pretended Kerry had said what he obviously had not. Only, the symbolic stick he (McCain) broke over Kerry's head came in a context even more disturbing. Mr. McCain demanded an apology while electioneering for a Republican congressional candidate in Illinois. He was speaking of how often he had been to Walter Reed Hospital to see the wounded Iraq veterans, of how 'many of them have lost limbs.' He said all this while demanding that the voters of Illinois reject a candidate who is not only a wounded Iraq veteran, *but who lost two limbs there,* (italics added) Tammy Duckworth."

Putting this remarkable event in context, John McCain knows firsthand of war as does Tammy Duckworth. In 1967, John McCain was piloting an A-4 Skyhawk when he was shot down over Truc Bach Lake, North Viet Nam. He was subsequently captured, tortured, bayoneted, and imprisoned at Hoa Lo Prison, the "Hanoi Hilton" where beatings, interrogation, and torture continued. This man's extraordinary courage is given an almost surreal dimension when one considers the following circumstance. John McCain's father was the Commander-in-Chief, Pacific Command, Commander of all U.S. forces in Viet Nam. When the North Viet Namese heard of this, John McCain was offered early repatriation. Due to his honor, and the honor he shared with his fellow prisoners, HE REFUSED

OUT-OF-TURN REPATRIATION. Thus John McCain waited 5 MORE YEARS before coming home. His conduct and heroism brought exemplary honor, above and beyond, to himself and to those with whom he served… seemingly until he was aware of democrat Tammy Duckworth.

The context becomes more remarkable when one considers that in the 2000 South Carolina Republican Presidential Primary, Senator McCain was the victim of his own cannibalistic party and its frontrunner George Bush. Push-polling is a tawdry way of influencing voters prior to casting a ballot. The innuendo-laden question of the primary that arguably doomed John McCain was, "Would you be more likely or less likely to vote for John McCain for president if you knew he had fathered an illegitimate black child?" Incidentally, the McCains, long before the primary, had adopted a Bangladeshi girl. Incidentally, Tammy Duckworth lost, and in the process…so did we.

Republicans and Democrats have prevented ballot initiatives that would threaten their bi-polar duopoly of power. In 1995 Ross Perot formed the Independence Party (subsequently the Reform Party). The Reform Party began an initiative to permit a ballot entry whereby a voter would not be forced to choose between the lesser of two evils offered by the parties, crammed down the throats of the electorate. A voter could elect the option of: "None Of The Above". Consequently the voter has the full power of referendum. The "None Of The Above" ballot choice would eliminate the forced acceptance of the lesser of two evils; "None Of The Above" permits full choice. Either/or means the electorate must choose from a menu of mediocrity. "None Of The Above" means they have to accept our mandate for excellence not pandering.

Ideologies and opportunistic intent fly under the radar screen of the electorate when legislation is compacted into omnibus bills. Bills are passed in this way by politicians who trade principle for expediency by the custom that one-hand-washes-the-other and in the process the electorate gets hosed. Legislation includes "earmark" spending (pork) on behalf of each scoundrel, and then each scoundrel can excuse his vote (for or against) by saying it was in relation to the greater part of the bill as a whole. This plausible deniability is abetted by polls that inform politicians what to say because they reveal what we want to hear. That comment aside, incumbents tell us want we want to hear, incumbents vote the way they want, and explain it away with the art of spin, only to repeat the process because the electorate has such a short memory. And two idiots can outvote a genius. It must be mentioned too that the ballot box or voting booth is the only place where the minimum wage worker has as much power as the CEO. CEO's use the same political impulse and determination to effect policy through lobbyists that they did to climb the corporate ladder. Workers at minimum wage generally lack the discipline and drive of the CEO and consequently are minimized in the overall process that governs the political spectrum.

In the United States, the two major parties have decided to monopolize the dynamic of elective politics because it's easier to slay one foe than many. Establishing any third party is a daunting endeavor that would challenge both wings of an establishment that is bought and paid for. The sole matter on which democrats and republicans agree is that there will be no other substantive party, no other substantive voice of governance to challenge their duopoly of power. When influence peddling is limited between two parties, corporate donors sponsor each party and play both against each other. The corporations "win" because win-or-lose they have bought influence with the "ins". Parties win because their coffers reek with dough. Lower and middle classes are fleeced to their britches. On the other side of the two party equation, influence peddlers and party fundraisers have been known to "shake down" potential donors and with this immoral behavior we are aghast at the leaders for whom we must settle.

When policy is influenced by favor, money, and the power-lust of incumbency, is it any wonder social security is in danger, that we face the looming catastrophe of global warming, that government looks askance at corruption, that we enter war for reasons of business under the guise of national security? When governmental administration and policy are not required to be efficient because they are insulated from the same market forces (i.e. competition) they publicly espouse, why are we shocked at budget deficits in the trillions of dollars? Professional politicians fund their existence using excessive taxation as a form of legalized theft. Taxation mollifies the twin monsters of bureaucratic inefficiency and waste, i.e. pork barrel spending (bringing home the bacon) because the whores and gigolos of congress have not the moral certitude of self-accountability or the discipline of self-governance. The sole difference between a diplomat or member of congress and a petty thief is that the thief hasn't the power to enact legislation to provide immunity from prosecution.

Power begins with money, tempts with favor, and acts through patronage. Patronage: the power to control appointments to office or the right to privileges. Rats who live the sewers of politics thrive on the slime of patronage. Without consideration to effort, merit or ability, those in power beknight the unqualified or unworthy, creating political capital (*dependency*) and in so doing, perpetuate mediocrity at best, graft and corruption at worst. Politics creates a we/they division between qualified and unqualified. We need not look any father than the Catholic Church for the ultimate expression of patronage. The church may not have invented patronage though it made patronage an art form when canonizing it. Even Patrick, the patron saint of Ireland, must acknowledge this blarney.

We/they, "ins/outs", also exist in the realm of spirituality yet they are not referred to as parties, they are called sects, denominations, and religions. The nests in which theological dogma is born, incubated and nurtured, is that of religion. People of influence amid religious communities divide the human family just as surely as politicians of government. Lack of understanding and intolerance abound between religions and between sects within religions. Intolerance causes conflict among those who practice heterosexual sex and those who practice the "abomination" of homosexual sex. Intolerance causes conflict between races and nations. Intolerance in the form of misogyny foments conflict between women and men.

Recently the most senior Muslim cleric in Australia gave a sermon, which is remarkably similar to the attitudes once expressed by Christian counterpart Saint Augustine. Quoting from Richard Kerbaj's article that appeared in The Australian on October 26, 2006, "In a Ramadan sermon that has outraged Muslim women leaders, Sydney-based Sheik Taj Din al-Hilali also alluded to the infamous Sydney gang rapes, suggesting the attackers were not entirely to blame. While not specifically referring to the rapes, brutal attacks on four women for which a group of young Lebanese men received long jail sentences, Sheik Hilali said there were women who "sway suggestively" and wore make-up and immodest dress..."and then you get a judge without mercy (rahma) and gives you 65 years."

"But the problem begins with who?" he asked. The leader of the [year of] 2000 rapes in Sydney's southwest, Bilal Skaf, a Muslim, was initially sentenced to 55 years' jail but later had the sentence reduced on appeal. In the religious address on adultery to about 500 worshippers in Sydney last month, Sheik Hilali commented: "If you take out uncovered meat and place it outside on the street, or in the garden or in the park, or in the backyard without a cover, and the cats come and eat it…whose fault is it, the cats or the uncovered meat? The uncovered meat is the problem." In the same article Mr. Kerbaj quotes the Sheik as having said that women were "weapons" used by "Satan" to control men. Someone capable of such hate and loathing is seemingly incapable of sharing love with a woman.

Though, in fairness, the west has its share of persons of particular paranoia. When speaking at the Conservative Political Action Conference on March 2, 2007, right-wing pundit Ann Coulter said: "I was going to have a few comments on the other Democratic presidential candidate John Edwards, but it turns out you have to go into rehab if you use the word "faggot," so I — so kind of an impasse, can't really talk about Edwards." Ms. Coulter is no different a verbal grenade thrower than Sheik al-Hilali, only she has different targets. Though in fact, vitriol generally betrays envy. Me thinks she doth protest too much. One may wonder why the homophobic Miss Coulter was silent about the sexuality of politically conservative reverend Ted Haggard and his ongoing relationship with a homosexual prostitute?

"In 401 A.D. Saint Augustine, bishop of Hippo, was one of the two most influential Catholic theologians ever. He wrote 'nothing is so powerful in drawing the spirit of a man downwards, as the caresses of a woman.'"[30] And certainly intolerance is borne with righteous indignation and directed against the wastrel of non-belief, the infidel.

CHAPTER 8
WHEREAS, DYSTOPIA...

"Until philosophers are kings, or the kings and princes of this world have the spirit and power of philosophy...cities will never cease from ill, nor the human race."
– Plato.

Two millennia later, English author and statesman, Sir Thomas More virtually echoes Plato, "Nations will be happy, when either philosophers become kings, or kings become philosophers." When 16th century Renaissance English writer Sir Thomas More wrote a book describing what he considered to be a perfect world, he called his perfect world, and his book, *Utopia*. Sir More's resume gave credence to his hypothesis. In 1517, at age 32, he was secretary and personal advisor to king Henry VIII. Six years later More became Speaker of the House of Commons and later served as high steward for both Cambridge and Oxford Universities. Four hundred years later Saint More was canonized by Pope Pius XI. "When Utopus founded Utopia, he made a law stating that no person should be punished for their religion, and that each man could be of whatever religion he pleased. Furthermore, only through persuasion and argument were people to influence others to join their religion. Thus, when one newly-Christian Utopian showed too much zeal and shouted words of bitterness against other religions, he was condemned to banishment, as was the law. The law also stated that such people could be condemned to slavery. The reason such laws were passed was because Utopus believed that God might have different ways of inspiring different men, and thus nobody should be punished for that. However, should there be only one true religion, that religion will become apparent through discourse and unprejudiced argument. Despite this, he did pass a law stating that nobody was allowed to think that the human soul died with the human body, or that the world was governed by chance."[31]

When speaking of civil governance, More states, "A conspiracy of the rich, who on pretence of managing the public only pursue their private ends, and devise all the ways and arts they can find out; first that they may, without danger, preserve all that they have so ill acquired, and then that they may engage the poor to toil and labor for them at so low rates as possible, and oppress them as they please. Utopians value everything God has given them, including their body, which they take good care of. They think it wrong and immoral to leave the body idle, ruining something that God has bestowed on them."

Politicians and ideologues of religion and governance use propaganda, ideology and dogma to coerce the Human Tabernacle to worship solely within the bounds of orthodox belief and approved doctrine. When More spoke of Utopia, he attempted to conceptualize a "perfect" state. The current condition of *spiritus mundi* indicates that mankind has achieved not the Utopia envisioned by Sir More, but rather Dystopia, a dysfunctional environment wracked with despair, selfish desire, materialism and emotional starvation. When considering Dystopia, one only has to acknowledge ongoing tragedies in Darfur, Zimbabwe, Sri Lanka, the Congo, North Korea, Myanmar, Nepal,

Rwanda, United States aggression in he Middle East, ad nauseum. Governmental politics and religious thought have been impotent in coping with, and indeed have exacerbated conditions that have wrought a contemporary Dystopia.

Our dystopic world contains "crack" infants, beggars who commit paedo-mutilation on their children to enhance their opportunities for larger donations, elder citizens assaulted for miniscule amounts of cash, child molesters, Hiv-aids, people who abandon babies, et cetera. Dystopia is perpetuated by communication media that endow the felon with notoriety and subsequently, in large part, ignores the works of the Good Samaritan. Dystopia is perpetuated when an electorate mortgages the future of their children by choosing politicians who purchase incumbency by promising more than they are able to deliver, or deliver more than is economically feasible...and the gullibility of the electorate who continually disregards precedent and believes the falsehoods of those running for office. Dystopians have an insatiable desire for physical and/or emotional violence. The following dichotomies exist within societies of today when this author envisions Utopia:

Whereas, in Dystopia, the desire to amass wealth, power, and possessions beyond reason is implemented with political connivance and sloth of effort, in Utopia nothing is free, everything is earned consequently nothing is owed. Utopians gladly give or receive consequently they do not owe or demand.

Whereas in Dystopia, elective political office is sought by those persons of dubious character with a carnal desire for power who tell any falsehood, commit any misdeed; in Utopia, according to Sir

More, "...anyone who deliberately tries to get himself elected to a public office is permanently disqualified from holding one."

Whereas, in Dystopia, citizenry connive at any level to obtain position or possession by political fiat; in Utopia, position and possession are earned by effort and merit alone.

Whereas, in Dystopia, stress, drugs, and violence, are sought and experienced as stimulants/barbiturates; in Utopia, reality is such that narcotics are not needed to vaccinate against a toxic society.

Whereas, in Dystopia, virtually all goods and services, materials and processes, research and development can be bought and sold on the open market (including those for which it is unlawful to do so); in Utopia, financial-value is prohibited id est nothing has cost and people are not faced with the necessity or desire to put a price tag on their souls/bodies low enough to attract a buyer/predator. In Utopia, morals, scruples, or principles are not subject to "mark down" to meet the voracious appetite of the capitalist carnivore.

Whereas, in Dystopia, the liar, thief, or cheater believe they have succeeded in cheating others; in Utopia, these cheaters would realize they have only cheated themselves.

Whereas, in Dystopia, people frivolously sue others to seek redress or compensation for their own faults or failures, Utopians have the self-esteem and dignity to consider this type of action reprehensible and the equivalent of moral fraud. Recently a person in Washington D.C. sued Jin and Soo Chung of Custom Cleaners for an allegedly misplaced $800.00 pair of pants. The plaintiff, Judge Roy Pearson, is seeking $67,000,000.00 in damages. One wonders why this Dystopian would need $800 pants, and why he would use his power to browbeat immigrants who were realizing their American dream? With no apparent sense of morality, what kind of justice would this man adjudicate?

Whereas, in Dystopia, the judicial system more often than not, favors the rights of the accused or convicted; in Utopia, justice would favor the victim. On March 6, 2007, I. Lewis "Scooter" Libby, Vice President Dick Cheney's former chief of staff, was convicted on charges of lying to government investigators undertaking the probe into the leaking of the name of CIA agent Valerie Plame. On March 6, 2007, Mr. Libby was convicted on two counts of perjury, one count of making false statements, and one of obstruction of justice. There were immediate calls from political conservatives calling for future if not immediate pardon. In Utopia, pardon is reserved for the innocent who were wrongly convicted.

Whereas, in Dystopia, the action of the whistleblower is ridiculed (not a team-player, disgruntled), or condemned (a rat); in Utopia, having the conscience to determine morality and the courage to honor that morality by shining light on illegal and/or immoral activity is applauded and encouraged. In Utopia, the message is not confused with the messenger.

Whereas, in Dystopia, insurers interpret premiums as their money, not as the client's money held in escrow, and crawl as low as possible to devise loopholes and seek innovative (and cruel) ways to abide only by the "*Letter*" of the policy in order to keep their money; in Utopia, the "*Spirit*" of the policy is realized and a client's claim to compensation is *honored*. Dystopia has realized Cicero's observation, "Summum ius summa iniuria" (more law less justice) because juris law is free from emotion.

Whereas in Dystopia, heroism is defined by a pentagon focused on propaganda (Psychological-Operations Unit) that must manufacture heroes to promote a disastrous war, in Utopia a woman such as Jessica Lynch displays more courage than her military chain-of-command when testifying before congress that her actions were not heroic.

In 1994, Michael P. Fay (charged with more than *50* counts of theft and vandalism) was found guilty in a court of law of a sovereign Singapore. He was sentenced to 4 months in jail, a fine of 3500 Singaporean dollars (US$ 2,214 at the time), and six lashes of the cane. President Bill Clinton and 24 senators pleaded for clemency from caning in which a rattan cane is used to thrash a subject who has been strapped to a metal frame, buttocks exposed. The cane is soaked in water (sometimes saltwater) to prevent splitting in order to maximize pain. Singaporeans had and continue to have a convincing case both against unwanted (and rightly unwelcome) American influence and hegemony and for a harsh penal system that makes their country safer than the one pleading clemency for the criminal. The American position would have had moral credence if it had advocated on behalf of the victims or had someone else felt so sorry for Mr. Fay as to emulate Damon and suffer his lashes. In the 4th century B.C. (according to legend) Pythias, a friend of Damon, was condemned to death by Dionysius the Elder and asked a respite to put his affairs in order; Damon knowing of Pythias' need, on his honor, pledged his life for the return of his friend. When Pythias returned at the prescribed time, and in so doing honoring Damon, the Tyrant released them both. Utopia is in dire need of citizens of honor and a Dionysius of wisdom.

Whereas, in Dystopia, televised media afford virtually any opportunity to maximize profit by offering the programming equivalent of a "twinkie" with purile, pedantic, offerings such as the Simpson's, voyeuristic titillation such as Survivor or American Idol, or an unending litany of violence that continually stoops to more craven depths to exhume ever more disgusting or revolting content; in Utopia, humor is still funny without vulgarity, story lines would actually have interesting plots and dialogue, and good Samaritans would be acknowledged rather than bestowing notoriety to the felon.

Whereas, in Dystopia, any effort is made and any position compromised to make a buck, in Utopia, financial value does not exist ergo there is no cost. In Dystopia, media advertisements accuse business people of being ***impotent*** (connectile disfunction) if they have an inadequate (understood to mean any company other than Sprint) broadband connection.

Whereas, in Dystopia, parents raise their children by remote control, and after its too late, blame educators for poorly educating their children, in Utopia, parents acknowledge and honor the responsibility of their children's education with day-to-day involvement. Whereas, in Dystopia, educators use "social grading" or succumb to grade inflation, which ultimately degrades achievement, in Utopia, grades are earned by quantity and quality of completed assignments of courses.

Whereas, in Dystopia, the *Contract of Matrimony* is most times a matter of the coupling of finance, convenience, circumstance (unwanted pregnancy), arrangement, or any confluences thereof, in Utopia, one reason, and one reason alone determines the *Bond of Marriage*, mutual love.

Whereas, in Dystopia, people who live in-utero for months are killed by ennui or discretion! Moral comas obfuscate the mind that is charged with the decision to render abortion. *Justifications* are used to excuse or anesthetize the conscience that involuntarily advocates for life. The "justification" that the child won't feel the pain is ludicrous. Whether or not this is the case, would you elect to end your life today without pain? Would you permit someone else to make that choice for you? Nobody of healthy, supple mind would answer these questions in the affirmative. In Utopia, life is sacrosanct, and no distinction is made whether in-utero or extra-utero. The fact of the matter (fair or not, justified upon fairness or not) is, that "a woman's right to choose" is best exercised when selecting the caliber of person with whom she wishes to be a sexual partner. It is heinous to reward promiscuity with abortion. An in-utero child, without even the dignity of a name, need not suffer chemical asphyxiation only to be tossed into a bio-sac and be disposed of like a used Kleenex.

Whereas in Dystopia, Dystopians die in wars that 'justify' triumph over an adversary, be the conflict over democracy or jihad; Utopians honor and value the sanctity of life over all else. The Utopian way of conflict expression is to target the enemy king *alone* with a huge reward that is *doubled* should the king be captured alive. Utopians regard for life is such that, "They're thinking of all the soldiers who would have been killed in action, on one side or the other – for they feel almost as much sympathy for the mass of the enemy population as they do for their own. They realize that these people would never have started a war if they hadn't been forced into it by the insanity of their rulers." – Thomas More, *Utopia*.

Quoting Utopia yet again, "They (Utopians) don't like bloody victories – in fact they feel ashamed of them, for they consider it stupid to pay too high a price for anything, however valuable it is. What they're really proud of is outwitting the enemy. They celebrate any success of this kind by a triumphal procession, and by putting up a trophy, as for some feat of heroism. You see, their idea of (ac)quitting themselves like men is to achieve victory by means of something which only man possesses, that is, by the power of the intellect. They say any animal can fight with its body – bears, lions, boars, wolves, dogs can all do it, and most of them are stronger and fiercer than we are – but what raises us above them is our reason and intelligence."

Whereas, in Dystopia, sexual expression is naughty and (ideally) should only occur under the aegis of church marriage with one person (for divorce was banned) of the opposite sex (never alone); in Utopia, a healthy vibrant libido is fully expressed, whose confines are those that exist between adults in full understanding consent.

Whereas, in Dystopia, the wealth of tithes rendered to the religious establishment serves first to provide succor and security to clergy, while most of the population of the planet live without adequate education, electricity, potable water, food, and in most cases, combinations of any or all of these; in Utopia, the sheep are fed before the shepherd.[j]

Whereas, in Dystopia, God punishes with vengeance; in Utopia, God/Allah/the Great Integrity/Mythras/Brahman nurtures with patience, understanding, and atonement.

---

[j] Blue Bell Ice Cream of Brenham, Texas, has a marvelously conceived slogan they use to market their ice cream, "We eat all we can and we sell the rest!" This type of attitude is quite humorous with Blue Bell regarding it's ice cream, but far less humorous in the context of the Vatican and it's money, or any established religion whose leaders comport in similar manner.

Whereas, in Dystopia, God/Allah is feared and the message of God/Allah (Bible and Qu'ran) has been hijacked just as surely and effectively as the four aircraft on September 11, 2001; in Utopia God/Allah/Mythras/Brahman is adored and the word of God/Allah is readily apparent in the affection and care extended to those we know and apparent in the patience and understanding we extend to those we know not.

Whereas in Dystopia; John 3:36, "He that believeth on the Son hath everlasting life: and he that believeth not the Son shall not see life; but the wrath of God abideth on him." and Surah 8:37, "That Allah may separate the wicked from the good, The wicked will He place piece upon piece, and heap them all together, and consign them unto hell. Such verily are the losers." Salvation (presumably from Hell), which is to say, the state of life in eternity, is *conditional* upon favor of church or the equally sinister favor of a wrathful God/Allah; in Utopia God's love is *unconditional*.

To the extent Homo Divinitas emulates unconditional love we emulate Divinity. A step toward Utopia is taken when any person helps another without expectation of compensation, a random act of kindness. Dikembe Mutombo was born in Kinshasa, Zaire. As a youth, young Dikembe sold trinkets amidst the street markets of Kinshasa and would gross an average of one dollar (US) per day. As an adult, Mr. Mutombo became a basketball star first at Georgetown University and subsequently in the National Basketball Association. As an adult, Mr. Mutombo donated 8 million dollars to construct a hospital in the city of his youth. The Mutombo's also adopted four children. Morgan Tsvangerai, of Harare, Zimbabwe, leads political opposition to the barbaric Robert Mugabe. President (His Excellency) Mugabe has eviscerated Zimbabwe's economy (February

2007 inflation rate at 1300%) and tortured and killed members of the opposition Movement for Democratic Change. Mr. Tsvangerai, largely unknown in the west, has valiantly suffered beatings, torture, and incarceration, in his courageous attempt to unseat Africa's worst despot.

Any government of Utopia would be privileged to have men of honor and principle such as Dikembe Mutombo and Morgan Tsvangerai in positions of authority. These Utopians have the courage to be generous of gift and the wisdom to recognize violence as a weapon of weakness.

The French philosopher and Nobel Peace Prize winner, Albert Schweitzer (1875-1965) may have had the most eloquent, yet simple, description of a Utopian, "A man is ethical only when life, as such, is sacred to him, that of plants and animals as that of his fellow men, and when he devotes himself helpfully to all life that is in need of help." The eighth century Indian monk Shantiveda taught, "All the suffering in the world arises out of wanting happiness for self. All happiness in the world arises out of wanting happiness for others." Gandhi's Satyagraha (achieving goals through non-violence) and Schweitzer's "Erfurcht vor dem Leben", (reverence for life) and the wisdom of such as Confucius and Shantiveda would be the pillars upon which Utopian society would be established.

What is of essential consequence and thus antithetical to religious dogma and interpersonal politics is that worship, adoration, love, thankfulness, be expressed under the aegis *only* of those influences that each individual deems appropriate and/or necessary. Eagles such as Messrs. Mutombo and Tsvangerai do not flock, they are found one by one. The song of worship is beautiful if sung with full heart whether as solo, duet, or choir, a capella or with accompaniment. The song need not be in tune for all have different voices, however, the song must be sung. The Times Of India, New Delhi, of February 19,2007 published the following e-mail Letter to the Editor from Shreekrishna N. Phadnis, 'Muslim pujari in Andhra Pradesh temple' (Jan 29) brings out the inner harmony among religions. President A.P.J. Abdul Kalaam has rightly said that we have to progress from religion to spirituality. Arnold Toynbee, after surveying the story of the human race, observed, "it is already becoming clear that a chapter which had a Western beginning will have to have an Indian ending if it is not to end in the self-destruction of the human race... India's priceless heritage is dharma (beyond religion), which dictates that the highest life is the life of service to one's own kind. Swami Vivekanand said, "The highest truth is this: God is present in all beings. They are his multiple forms. There is no other God to seek. The first of all worship is the worship of those around us... He alone serves God who serves all other beings. The old faith and old culture of India are not merely for Hindus, not merely for India but for the whole world." Homo Divinitas must turn the tide from Dystopia to Utopia. We must serve God by serving all other beings.

The Upanishads (Hindu scripture) say: "All this is verily the Atman. The One, blissful Self indwells all beings." The spiritual oneness of all humanity is a great lesson that mankind (spiritus mundi) yearns for today. Whatever has been and whatever will be in the future, all this is verily the one, eternal Being alone. The Message of Divine Life is: See God in all faces. Serve all and love all with kindness, compassion, and empathy. Feel everyone to be your own. Serve your fellow beings in the spirit of worship offered to the Divine, which dwells within each of them. Service of man is truly the worship of God.

CHAPTER 9
REACHING FOR GOD

"You don't have a soul. You are a soul. You have a body."
– Clive Staples Lewis.

"Once I filled my hand with mist. Then I opened it and lo, the mist was a worm. And I closed and opened my hand again, and behold there was a bird. And again I closed and opened my hand, and in its hollow stood a man with a sad face, turned upward. And again I closed my hand, and when I opened it there was naught but mist. But I heard a song of exceeding sweetness."
- Kahlil Gibran.

Ashes to ashes, dust to dust, our eternal spiritual being is encased in corporeal clay, yet so often, the term "I" is identified with clay as the point of reference. Eternal souls are eternal life not the clay that mummifies them. Souls are bound by dimension upon the assumption of physical presence in earthly incarnation at the moment of conception. Such bounds persist until physical presence ends with death. Everyone wants to get to heaven but nobody wants to die, yet, just when the caterpillar thought the world was over, it became a butterfly. Eternal life is experienced without the constraint or warp of sensory perception. Souls that incarnate into dimension use bodily senses such as taste, smell, touch, hearing and vision to act as conduits that render interpretation and measure a state of existence (reality) within the dimensions of time and space. Senses have much to do with sensation however; they have little to do with Truth. A case in point, pilots who fly aircraft during clear weather may file a flight plan using Visual Flight Rules (VFR). In so doing, the pilot is required to maintain aircraft separation solely by line-of-sight. Pilots who fly during inclement weather file a flight plan using Instrument Flight Rules (IFR). When flying IFR, pilots use instruments to monitor all aspects of flight. Pilots are instructed (almost from birth) to trust and rely on instrument readings for position, attitude, and orientation. Pilots know their instruments are more reliable than their senses because senses, for lack of a better term, lie.

Unreliability and capriciousness of the senses is by no means a newly acknowledged concept. The Greek philosopher Democritus was born at Abdera, in Thrace circa 460 B.C. Democritus was a metaphysician who is most notable for the Atomism school of thought and was quite direct in his epistemological critique of knowledge (gnosis). Quoting Democritus, "There are two forms of knowledge: one legitimate, one bastard. To the bastard sort belong all the following: sight, hearing, smell, taste, touch. The legitimate is quite distinct from this. When the bastard form cannot see more minutely, nor hear nor smell nor taste nor perceive through the touch, then another finer form must be employed. – *The Symmetry of Life, Fragment 11*. The "finer form" to which Democritus refers is "reasoning" though "reason" is not explained in the atomistic view.

A formally recognized condition of sensory disorientation is known as vertigo. Another type of vertigo exists, that of spiritual vertigo. Man's natural tendency is toward freedom and independence. Spiritual vertigo occurs when senses belie natural tendencies and heed the distortion of, for lack of a better term, temptation, thereby causing the siren call of addiction to be answered by the courtship of the whore of dependence. Senses belie our spirits when opinions are formed, or judgments made, about *who* someone is when we consider only *what* they *seem* to be, i.e. body color, body shape or size, or the geography whence they came. Senses belie spirituality when someone else is perceived as ugly or beautiful. Spiritual vertigo occurs when we project self-held negatives upon another, and in so doing, assume those negatives to be theirs and not our own. Though the Constitution of the United States of America claims that "all men are created equal", such equality exists from the perspective of juris law. No two people are the same. How similarities and differences are viewed is more of a reflection of ourselves than those upon whom we cast fallacious perception and/or judgment.

The five tactile senses of awareness, taste, smell, touch, hearing, and vision, compete with the most complex sense of awareness, the conscience. Occasionally, the five senses, all of which can be responsive to "ego", may convey hurt, insecurity, greed, hunger, fear, desire, etc. These sensory feelings, at any given moment, may overwhelm the sense of conscience, which, is the infinite essence of being. "The soul is the mirror of an indestructible universe." – Gottfried Wilhelm Liebnitz (1646 -1716).

Though benign, senses are capable of misinterpretation or deceit, and often respond to ego as opposed to self. Organized religion, perhaps malignantly, compounds deception when using established religious texts to pander to their select market shares by portraying heaven as the satisfaction and culmination of the sensory desire they legislate against or prohibit on earth. Indeed, the Final Judgment (against "sinners") about which the Book of Revelation speaks, is yearned for, and referred to by fundamentalist evangelical Christians, as the

"Rapture". Is the term "rapture" a spiritual death wish or some sort of latent spiritual desire congruent with sensory (sensual) orgasm?

Organized religion causes and perpetuates spiritual vertigo when it touts a rapturous episode and exploits a view of heaven that provides sensory pleasures forbidden on earth. This spiritual con game causes and perpetuates schizophrenia of spiritus mundi that results in the friction of perpetual conflict and violence. The following quote by Kahlil Gibran puts life in a more wholesome context than most canonized scripture, "They say to me, "You must needs choose between the pleasures of this world and the peace of the next world." And I say to them, "I have chosen both the delights of this world and the peace of the next. For I know in my heart that the Supreme Poet wrote but one poem, and it scans perfectly, and it also rhymes perfectly.[32] Whether Paul, Jerome, Tertullian, Irenaus, Augustine, Benedict, Mohammed, continuing through Girolamo Savonarola (1452-1498) and Josemaria Escriva (1902-1975), all would be unable to recognize the wisdom of the Lebanese poet.

Friar Savonarola indeed initiated the so-called, Bonfire of the Vanities in 1497 in the Piazza della Signoria in Florence, whereby he and his followers collected mirrors, gaming tables, musical instruments, paintings (some by the genius Sandro Botticelli himself), cosmetics, lewd pictures and made a bonfire of those symbols of vanity. These selfsame bonfires existed prior to that of Savonarola however they consumed the oxygen of spiritual sovereignty itself from believers drawn by the flames of rabid religious fervor. Though Friar Savonarola preached in favor of the Christian life and was not making war against the church establishment, he preached without abandon against its transgressions. On May 13, 1497, Pope Alexander VI excommunicated Friar Savonarola. Predictably, excommunication was not enough however, as he was tortured, made to sign a confession, and was executed on May 23, 1498.

Consider that eternity, by definition, is devoid of matter and/or time. It therefore follows that senses are an oxymoron when considered in the context of infinity. Within the world of the finite, senses provide Homo Divinitas a way to experience life, and thereby, to express essence of spirit (conscience) within the dimensional world. In the realm of dimension, senses help determine parameters of behavior regarding the conduct of human endeavor as it relates to the equation of "reality"-based consequences. Words and actions of honor or disgrace, fidelity or betrayal, honesty or deception, regarding others, our environment, and ourselves bear immutable witness to, and are the truest measure of, consequences of the quest for unification with conscience, with Truth. Finishing the allegory presented earlier when speaking of flight, one may consider that when flying in stormy weather or any weather at all for that matter, it is best to use and rely on the most integral instrument of all, conscience. "Conscience is God's presence in man." – Emanuel Swedenborg.

"Free will" is the palette with which we paint self-portraits of honor, dignity, integrity, patience, compassion, and forgiveness. People also may favor undisciplined expedience, sloth, deceit, selfishness and hate. The universe renders opportunities and choices within which, we may determine destiny. We, each of us, are responsible for the sum of choices we make and how those same choices affect others. Karmic Law, for those who have ears to listen, seems to indicate we should begin making choices more in tune with a destiny of moral and ethical certitude as opposed to religious threat and reward. Infinite moral and ethical absolutes (Truths) are not subject to change even though they co-exist within the finite dimension of time and space. Politics in the form of practicalities, justifications, and rationalizations all of which are subject to sensory influence, attempt to compromise or excuse Truth. Nevertheless, we must realize moral and ethical absolutes for what they are and endeavor to emulate those absolutes, for it is that part of us which represents our reach for divinity. Now more than ever, it is necessary to pay heed to infinite moral and ethical ideals as opposed to the sensory temptations of the finite.

Emulating divinity, reaching for God, can occasionally best be illustrated by example. The following two extraordinary albeit unorthodox and entirely compelling stories will provide examples of all consuming love. In fact one would be hard-pressed to experience, or be aware of the deepest fathoms of love, which the following stories represent. Indeed this author was not aware of, and ventures to say that most readers have not or perhaps for that matter, cannot identify with, the emotion of the following stories. The love of a spouse, a son or daughter, grandson or granddaughter, are entirely rewarding and are in some respects the reason for the nature of our existence. These tales tell of a love that transcends affection and desire and goes to the core of our spiritual essence, the love of and desire to be one with the Great Integrity.

The first narrative comes from Karen Armstrong's superlative book, *A History of God* as she speaks of Jews and the holocaust. (Be prepared, because it involves a particularly gruesome incident from the holocaust.) "For many Jews, the traditional idea of God would become an impossibility after the Holocaust. The Nobel Prize winner Elie Wiesel had lived only for God during his childhood in Hungary; his life had been shaped by the disciplines of the Talmud, and he had hoped one day to be invited into the mysteries of the Kabbalah. As a boy, he was taken to Auschwitz and later to Buchenwald. During his first night in the death camp, watching the black smoke coiling to the sky from the crematorium where the bodies of his mother and sister were to be thrown, he knew that the flames had consumed his faith forever. He was in a world, which was the objective correlative of the Godless world imagined by Nietzsche. "Never should I forget that nocturnal silence which deprived me for all eternity, of the desire to live." He wrote years later. "Never shall I forget these moments which murdered my God and my soul and turned my dreams to dust." One day the Gestapo hanged a child. Even the SS were disturbed by the prospect of hanging a young boy in front of thousands of spectators. The child who, Wiesel recalled, had the face of a "sad-eyed angel," was silent, lividly pale and almost calm as he ascended the gallows. Behind Wiesel, one of the other prisoners asked: Where is God? Where is He?" It took the child half an hour to die, while the prisoners were forced to look him in the face. The same man asked again: Where is God now?" And Wiesel heard a voice within him make this answer: Where is He? Here He is – He is hanging here on this gallows." Dostoevsky had said that the death of a single child could make God unacceptable, but even he, no stranger to inhumanity had not imagined the death of a child in such circumstances. The horror of Auschwitz is a stark challenge to many more of the conventional ideas of God."[33] And yet, Ms. Armstrong continues, "Yet it is also true, that even in Auschwitz some Jews continued to study the Talmud and observe the traditional festivals, not because they hoped that God would rescue them but because it made sense. There is a story that one day in Auschwitz, a group of Jews put God on trial. They charged him with cruelty and betrayal. Like Job, they found no consolation in the usual answers to the problem of evil and suffering in the midst of this current obscenity.

They could find no excuse for God, no extenuating circumstances, so they found him guilty and, presumably, worthy of death. The Rabbi pronounced the verdict. Then he looked up and said that the trial was over: it was time for the evening prayer."[34] This author has never read of a more profound belief. I stand in awe of their magnificent belief and pray that in my small challenges, I can learn from their courage.

The second account concerns not so much the joy of attainment of love and worship so much as the despair of not knowing how to love and worship. If one looks closely and carefully at Friedrich Nietzsche, who once declared "God is Dead", it is not difficult at all to recognize that what may have driven a brilliant man to madness was his inability to love his God whom he so desperately sought. Quoting Nietzsche in *Also Spake Zarathustra* as Zarathustra pleads to God for His return:

No! come back,
With all your torments!
Oh come back
To the last of all solitaries!
All the streams of my tears
Run their course for you!
And the last flame of my heart –
It burns up to *you*!
Oh come back
My unknown God. My pain! My last – happiness.[35]

One may speculate that Nietzsche, brilliant though he was, and questioning all else, did not question religious leaders such as Augustine, Tertullian, and Irenaeus as incorporated in Christian dogma or perhaps the like of Jacob Frank of 18ᵗʰ century Askenazic Judaism. These men were just as guilty of killing the true message of Divinity as the Gestapo at Auschwitz. Furthermore, Herr Nietzsche's philosophic viewpoint is even more profound considering his father and both grandfathers were Lutheran ministers.

People who believe God is dead or people who consider themselves atheist or agnostic, may wish to consider the following anecdote making its way through cyberspace on the Internet. The author seems to be anonymous because no author's name is appended to the story. Nevertheless the concept is significant:

When You Thought I Wasn't Looking
Written by a former child.

A message every adult should read, because children are watching you and doing as you do, not as you say.
When you thought I wasn't looking, I saw you hang my
First painting on the refrigerator, and I immediately wanted to paint another one.
When you thought I wasn't looking I saw you feed a stray cat,
And I learned that it was good to be kind to animals.
When you thought I wasn't looking, I saw you make my favorite cake for me
And I learned that the little things can be the special things in life.
When you thought I wasn't looking, I heard you say a prayer,
 And I knew there is a God I could always talk to and I learned to trust in God.
When you thought I wasn't looking, I saw you make a meal and take it to a friend who was sick, and I learned that we all have to help take care of each other.

When you thought I wasn't looking, I saw you give of your time and money

To help people who had nothing and I learned that those who have something

Should give to those who don't.

When you thought I wasn't looking, I saw you take care of our house and everyone in it, and I learned that we have to take care of what we are given.

When you thought I wasn't looking, I saw how you handled your responsibilities, even when you didn't feel good and I learned that I would have to be responsible when I grow up.

When you thought I wasn't looking, I saw tears come from your eyes and I learned that sometimes things can hurt, but it's all right to cry.

When you thought I wasn't looking, I saw that you cared and I wanted to be everything that I could be.

When you thought I wasn't looking, I learned most of life's lessons that I need to know to be a good and productive citizen when I grow up.

When you thought I wasn't looking, I looked at you and wanted to say, "Thanks for all the things I saw when you thought I wasn't looking."

The author finishes by saying, "I am sending this to all of the people I know who do so much for others that think no one ever sees. Little eyes see a lot. Each of us (parent, grandparent, aunt, uncle, teacher, or friend) influences the life of a child."

When observing ourselves, and the world we create, please consider the context of that verse supposing the eyes silently watching are those of the Great Integrity (God/Allah). Atheists or agnostics, please consider this emotional overlay is just as appropriate as to how we treat our children, family, and friends, as to how Divinity perceives us. To members of organized religions who bicker and proselytize between sects, denominations, and religions, please consider that spiritual wholeness is available to all who choose to seek and the answer is not "one size fits all".

With the advent of the global village and the opportunities afforded by international travel and the internet our search and thus our spiritual scope can be expanded by becoming familiar with spiritual thought of the east as well as philosophies to which we have not yet been exposed, if only to more directly focus on that which we have adopted as personal belief.

Another generic anecdote is wending its way through the Internet, again attributable to no particular author, speaking of faith, of reaching to God:

An atheist professor of philosophy speaks to his class on the problem science has with God, the Almighty. He asks one of his new Christian student to stand and...

Professor: You are a Christian, aren't you son?
Student: Yes sir.
Prof: So you believe in God?
Student: Absolutely sir.
Prof: Is God good?
Student: Sure.
Prof: Is God all-powerful?
Student: Yes.

Prof: My brother died of cancer, even though he prayed to God to heal him. Most of us would attempt to help others who are ill. But God didn't. How is this God good then? Hmm? (Student is silent.)

Prof: You can't answer that can you? Let's start again young fella. Is God good?

Student: Yes.

Prof: Is Satan good?

Student: No.

Prof: Where does Satan come from?

Student: From…God.

Prof: That's right. Tell me son, is there evil in this world?

Student: Yes.

Prof: Evil is everywhere isn't it? And God did make everything. Correct?

Student: Yes.

Prof: So who created evil?

(Student does not answer.)

Prof: Is there sickness? Immorality? Hatred? Ugliness? All these terrible things exist in the world don't they?

Student: Yes sir.

Prof: So, who created them?

(Student has no answer)

Prof: Science says you have five senses you can use to identify and observe the world around you. Tell me son, have you ever seen God?

Student: No sir.

Prof: Tell us if you have ever heard your God?

Student: No sir.

Prof: Have you ever felt your God, tasted your God, smelt your God? Have you ever had any sensory perception of God for that matter?

Student: No sir. I'm afraid I haven't.

Prof: Yet you still believe in Him?

Student: Yes.

Prof: According to empirical, testable, demonstrable protocol, science says your God doesn't exist. What do you say to that, son?

Student: Nothing, I only have my faith.

Prof: Yes. Faith. And that is the problem science has.

Student: Professor, is there such a thing as heat?

Prof: Yes.

Student: And is there such a thing as cold?

Prof: Yes.

Student: No sir, there isn't.

(The lecture theatre becomes very quite at this turn of events.)

Student: Sir, you can have lots of heat, even more heat, superheat, megaheat, white heat, a little heat or no heat. But we don't have anything called cold. We can hit 458 degrees below zero, which is no heat, but we can't go any further after that. There is no such thing as cold. Cold is only a word we use to describe the absence of heat. We cannot measure cold. Heat is energy. Cold is not the opposite of heat, sir, just the absence of it.

(There is pin-drop silence in the lecture theatre.)

Student: What about darkness, Professor? Is there such a thing as darkness?

Prof: Yes. What is night if there isn't darkness?

Student: You're wrong again, sir. Darkness is the absence of something. You can have low light, normal light, bright light, flashing light... But if you have no light constantly, you have nothing and it's called darkness, isn't it? In reality, darkness isn't. If it were you would be able to make darkness darker, wouldn't you?

Prof: So what is the point you are making young man?

Student: Sir, my point is that your philosophical premise is flawed.

Prof: Flawed? Can you explain how?

Student: Sir, you are working on the premise of duality. You argue there is life and then there is death, a good God and a bad God. You are viewing the concept of God as something finite, something we can measure. Sir, science can't even explain a thought. It uses electricity and magnetism, but has never seen, much less fully understood either one. To view death as the opposite of life is to be ignorant of the fact that death cannot exist as a substantive thing. Death is not the opposite of life: just the absence of it. Now tell me, Professor. Do you teach your students that they evolved from a monkey?

Prof: If you are referring to the natural evolutionary process, yes, of course I do.

Student: Have you ever observed evolution with your own eyes, sir?

(The professor shakes his head with a smile, beginning to realize where the argument was going.)

Student: Since no one has ever observed the process of evolution at work and cannot even prove that this process is an on-going endeavor, are you not teaching your opinion, sir? Are you not a scientist, but a preacher?

(The class is in uproar.)

Student: Is there anyone in the class who has ever seen the Professor's brain?

(The class breaks out into laughter.)

Student: Is there anyone here who has ever heard the Professor's brain, felt it, touched or smelt it? ... No one appears to have done so. So, according to the established rules of empirical, stable, demonstrable protocol, science says that you have no brain, sir. With all due respect, sir, how do we then trust your lectures, sir?

(The room is silent. The professor stares at the student, his face unfathomable.)

Prof: I guess you'll have to take them on faith, son.

Student: That is it sir. The link between mankind and God is faith. That is all that keeps things moving and alive.

Please consider that the student's words could have been spoken by a Christian, a Muslim, a Buddhist, *anyone*. Faith, the upward reach to meet with Divinity is a seed that rests in all of mankind, perhaps dormant in some, yet existent nevertheless.

The author of this book has a dear friend who gives generously of his time, affection, and financial resources. He (and his wife of 55 years) gives to those friends who have genuine need. He is a man true to his word and though occasionally cantankerous, is one of the finest men I have ever known. This man believes only in the possibility there may be a Divine Creator, which makes his giving all the more profound. This man is more Christian than most Christians because he expects no eternal compensation for his good works. His (and her) heart is a giving and understanding heart and I am privileged to be considered as their friend. This then, presents an interesting dynamic. Surely, this gentleman never considered I would write a book, let alone mention him in it. Please bear in mind then, that should the person reading this book be remembered in a book by a future writer, how would the reader be referred to in that book? Further, please understand that there is a book being written by a divine Author. How do we wish to be remembered in that karmic book of infinity? Verily, the book is being written.

Another wonderful story has recently been relayed through the Internet about a young boy who was born to an unwed mother. It goes like this, " A seminary professor was vacationing with his wife in Gatlinburg, Tennessee. One morning, they were eating breakfast in a little restaurant, hoping to enjoy a quiet family meal. While they were waiting for their food, they noticed a distinguished looking, white-haired man moving from table to table visiting with the guests. The professor leaned over and whispered to his wife, "I hope he doesn't come over here." But sure enough, the man did come over to their table. "Where are you folks from?" he asked in a friendly voice. "Oklahoma", they answered. "Great to have you here in Tennessee," the stranger said. "What do you do for a living?" "I teach at a seminary." He replied. "Oh, so you teach preachers how to preach, do you? Well. I've got a really good story for you." And with that, the gentleman pulled up a chair and sat down at the table with the couple. The professor groaned and thought to himself, "great…just what I need – another preacher story!" The man started, "See that mountain over there?" (Pointing out a restaurant window). "Not far from the base of that mountain, there was a boy born to an unwed mother. He had a hard time growing up, because every place he went, he was always asked the same question, "Hey boy, who's your daddy?" Whether he was at school, in the grocery store or drug store, people would ask the same question. "Who's your daddy?"

He would hide at recess and lunchtime from other students. He would avoid going into stores because the question always hurt him so bad. When he was about 12 years old, a new preacher came to his church. He would always go in late and slip out early to avoid hearing the question. "Who's your daddy?" But one day, the new preacher said the benediction so fast, he got caught and had to walk out with the crowd. Just about the time he got to the back door the new preacher, not knowing anything about him, put his hand on his shoulder and asked him. "Son, who's your daddy?"

The church got deathly quiet. He could feel every eye in the church looking at him. Now everyone would finally know the answer to the question, "Who's your daddy?" The new preacher though, sensed the situation around him and using discernment that only the Holy Spirit could give, said the following to the scared little boy. "Wait a minute!" I know who you are. I see the family resemblance now. You are a child of God." With that, he patted the boy on his shoulder and said, "Boy, you've got a great inheritance, go and claim it." With that, the boy smiled for the first time in a long time and walked out the door a changed person. He was never the same again. Whenever anybody asked him, "Who's your daddy?" he'd just tell them, "I'm a child of God." The distinguished gentleman got up from the table and said, "Isn't that a great story?" The professor responded that it really was a great story. As the man turned to leave, he said. "You know, if that new preacher hadn't told me that I was one of God's children, I probably would never have amounted to anything." And he walked away.

The seminary professor and his wife were stunned. He called the waitress over and asked her, "Do you know that man who just left that was sitting at our table?" The waitress grinned and said, "Of course. Everybody here knows him. That's Ben Hooper. He's the former Governor of Tennessee!"

Someone in your life today needs a reminder they are one of God's children.

Reaching for God is a self-help program, but it can be more effective when it helps to benefit and influence people around us. Reaching for God can have results when we boost another child of God one step higher in their search. And make no mistake; no matter the age; with the backdrop of infinity, we are always as children because infinity has no element of time. The story is told of the student who, when enrolling in university, did so to emulate his master, unaware at his young age that a true master is ever emulating the student.

On earth, corporeal bodies may show the effects of age (time) yet souls are incorporeal, thus without age. On earth, skin may have different colors, yet souls are essential (of essence, and therefore have no color). On earth, physical beauty (as curse or blessing) has absolutely nothing to do with who we are, and outward appearance has nothing to do with our personage in the hereafter. Beauty is not defined by shape of face or body. Beauty is defined by who we are and what we do (create) as opposed to what we look like, i.e. our appearance; how we appear to be. Should people put as much effort and energy into creating beautiful deeds instead of appearing beautiful with face-lifts, tummy-tucks, liposuction, and botox, people would be beautiful as opposed to appearing beautiful. "Beauty is worse than wine, it intoxicates both the holder and beholder." – Aldous Huxley.

Beauty should not be confused with goodness. Someone who possesses superficial outward beauty can lie and steal. A person who possesses inner beauty of spirit will seldom lie or steal. Beauty manifests when predicated on the self-perception of self-esteem earned by the discipline of moral and ethical choice vis-à-vis ourselves, and our inter-reactions with others. Beauty is by nature a subjective abstract concept that is best realized and appreciated when self-determined, self-directed, and self-applied. Also, beauty is not a caveat for admission into, or state of being in, heaven. Were that the case, God would be just as faulted with vanity as the same vain human beings who emulate "Him". Another instance of creating God in our image, or is it the other way around? It is interesting to note French enlightenment writer and philosopher Voltaire (1694-1778), "If God created us in His own image, we have more than reciprocated."

When considering Who created Whom and how each is perceived, please consider the perspective of Saint Jerome. Jerome (Latin: Eusebius Sophronius Hieronymus) (circa 347 – 420) was honored in 1298 as one of the four Great Doctors of the Western Church. Over a period of 15-18 years, Jerome, a learned scholar, was responsible for the translation of the Bible into Latin from its original Greek and Hebrew texts. This translation, the Vulgate Bible, is so termed from the Latin vulgatus: vulgar (which is to say, common). To appreciate the context and perspective of someone who would undertake and formalize such significant work, or any work for that matter, one must be aware of how an author views the world in which he lives. St. Jerome, "condemns the marriage of priests and their sexual digressions, and argues powerfully for clerical celibacy; only monks, he thinks, are true Christians, free from property, lust, and pride. With an eloquence that would have enlisted Casanova, Jerome calls upon men to give up all and follow Christ, asks the Christian matrons to dedicate their first-born to the Lord as offerings due under the Law, and advises his lady friends, if they cannot enter a convent, at least to live as virgins in their homes. He comes close to rating marriage as sin. "I praise marriage, but because it produces me virgins"; he proposes to "cut down by the ax of virginity the wood of marriage." And exalts John the celibate apostle over Peter, who had a wife."[36]

Perhaps the vitriol with which Jerome portrays catholic thought is a reflection of the pain of having been reproved (at an early age) by his bishop as being overly intolerant. Forced to leave the brotherhood he helped found, he eventually chose the life of an anchorite in a desert hermitage with his library (containing Cicero and Virgil) with him. While a hermit, Jerome's epiphany came to him in a dream as he was, "dragged before the Judge's judgment seat. I was asked to state my condition, and replied that I was a Christian. But He Who presided said, "thou liest; thou art a Ciceronian, not a Christian. For where thy treasure is, there will thy heart be also." Straightaway, I became dumb. And [then I felt] the strokes of the whip – for He had ordered me to be scourged…. At last the bystanders fell at the knees of Him Who presided, and prayed Him to pardon my youth and give me an opportunity to repent of my error, on the understanding that the extreme of torture should be inflicted upon me if I ever read again the books of Gentile authors…. This experience was no sweet or idle dream…. I profess that my shoulders were black and blue, and that I felt the bruises long after I awoke…. Henceforth I read the books of God with greater zeal than I had ever given before to the books of men."[37]

The underlying scourge of Jerome's self-contempt would seem to be his aversion to knowledge and learning. British philosopher Bertrand Russell (1872-1970) once remarked, "A stupid man's report of what a clever man says is never accurate because he unconsciously translates what he hears into something he can't understand." Russell's seeming condescension notwithstanding, his basic premise is accurate.

Buddha spoke of a different sort of sensory misperception other than the "vertigo" referred to herein, "The world, indeed, is like a dream and the treasures of the world are an alluring mirage! Like the apparent distances in a picture, things have no reality in themselves, but they are like heat haze." St. Jerome was far from stupid yet his antipathy has become ecclesiastical heritage. Jerome was a victim of spiritual vertigo of the heat haze (of masochism) that Buddha described centuries before Jerome.

Another instance of fear and loathing was evident in Saint Benedict. When Jerome counseled that "only monks are true Christians", he may have idealized someone such as Benedict (circa 480-543) of Nursia. Saint Benedict founded Monte Cassino, the most famous monastery in Latin Christendom. Having, at 15 years of age, suffered the ignominy of love and love lost, he fled and spent several years as a solitary monk. "The *Dialogues* of Pope Gregory I tell how Benedict fought valiantly to forget the woman... the memory of whom the wicked spirit put into his mind, and by that memory so mightily inflamed with concupiscence the soul of God's servant...that, almost overcome with pleasure, he was of a mind to forsake the wilderness. But suddenly, assisted by God's grace, he came to himself; and by seeing many thick briers and nettle bushes growing hard by, off he cast his apparel, and threw himself into the midst of them, and there wallowed so long that when he rose up all his flesh was pitifully torn; and so by the wounds of his body, he cured the wounds of his soul."[38]

"Mortification is by no means the centerpiece of the Christian life, but nobody can grow closer to God without it: There is no holiness without renunciation and spiritual battle." (Catechism of the Catholic Church, n. 2015).

"In fact, the law requires that nearly everything be cleansed with blood, and without the shedding of blood there is no forgiveness." – Hebrews (9:22).

St. Jerome lived in fear of knowledge and learning and St. Benedict (the Benedictine Order) lived in fear of love. When the church canonized these men it also canonized their sado-masochistic beliefs. It may be said that Jerome, Benedict, Tertullian, Augustine, St. Paul, Mohammed, et al, expressed love (in the form of worship) by virtue of prodigious intellect. Though virtue did not end there, these men and many others who established organized religion, seem unable to communicate using the love of their hearts and quite apparently, unable to identify, embrace, and express heart-felt love (Eros) with their bodies.

Hypothetical questions find only hypothetical answers. Nevertheless, this author wonders what men such as St. Augustine, Tertullian, et al, would glean from the following letter written by Bachendri Pal as told to S. Shanthi which appeared in the Sunday Times Of India (Lucknow, February 25, 2007), "God is in my thoughts, my feelings and my mind. I believe in helping others and finding God in my service. As a child I used to visit temples very often, do *mannatein*, fast for the well being of others and everything I could possibly do to reach God. However, as I grew up I realized that I don't have to visit religious places to find God. Today, I find Him in helping the elderly, my empathy toward animals and everything I do for others. My family members are very religious. My sister is totally into *puja path* and other rituals. I often tell her that if you help others and be nice to them you will find God. I am not saying that rituals are bad. I believe every person has the right to do what he or she wants, but you should remember that just going to a temple or mosque is not going to solve your problems. I am thankful to God not because I climbed Mount Everest but because He has given me strength to take the right decisions in life and help others as much as I can. Being honest gives you the power to succeed in life. It makes you strong. Recently, I met with an accident and the doctor had asked me to take bed rest. But I had some commitments and was confused what to do. That was the time when the voice inside me said that nothing would happen to me, as I have never done any harm to anyone in life. I went ahead with my plans and I was right – nothing happened to me. The only time I felt bad was when my father died. I was very close to him and was feeling guilty that I couldn't spend much time with him. I believe in simple living and high thinking. I have not forgotten my roots. I know where I come from and do my best to help everyone to succeed in life. I love myself and I believe it's very important to love yourself."

When considering Who created Whom, one may strongly posit that each is part and parcel of the other and that religion has done a miserable job of representing Divinity while Divinity did a magnificent job of creating Homo Divinitas and the universe we inhabit and cohabit. Walt Disney and his team of animators more accurately anthropomorphized Mickey Mouse and his menagerie of friends than Judaic, Islamic, and Christian religious leaders have done anthropomorphizing God/Allah/Yahweh, His saints, and prophets. Mr. Disney said, "Animation can explain whatever the mind of mankind can conceive. This faculty makes it the most versatile and explicit means of communication yet derived for quick mass appreciation." Walt Disney applied animation to mice (Mickey Mouse and Minnie), dogs (Pluto), and human character (Snow White, et cetera) and in doing so, created a world of wonder and wholesome value. The engineers of early pan-societal religious doctrine animated Deity with wrath, vengeance, pettiness, ad nauseum. The church, which in this context means all of organized religion, has been engineered into, and remains on, a course that renders unto itself all that was meant for Caesar; influence, power, and wealth, at the spiritual expense of believers it presumes to offer salvation. Augustine, Tertullian, Irenaeus, Benedict, et cetera, all the usual suspects are revered and most have been canonized. Walt Disney remains loved and bequeathed a legacy of happiness to children of all ages. Mr. Disney will never be ecclesiastically canonized, however he will be canonized by the happiness in the hearts of children and parents for aeons to follow.

CHAPTER 10
LOVE

Verse 99, The Rubaiyat, by Omar Khayyam:
"Ah. Love. Could you and I with Him conspire
To grasp this sorry Scheme of Things entire,
Would not we shatter it to bits – and then
Re-mould it nearer to the Heart's Desire!"

"I met in the street a very poor young man who was in love. His
hat was old, his coat worn, his cloak was out at the elbows, the
water passed through his shoes, - and the stars through his soul."
– Victor Hugo.

Though mankind has searched for thousands of years to clumsily though nobly attempt to define love, it is impossible to describe infinite love with finite vocabulary. A remarkable difference between love and hate is that love nourishes lover and beloved as opposed to hate, which consumes the hater not the hated. Indifference is the opposite of love, not hate. The act of feeling and expressing love is an attempt to emulate the Great Integrity; hate is a form of self-abuse. "Omnia vincit Amor; et nos cedamus Amori" – Virgil *Eclogues*, X. "Love conquers all; let us too yield to love"…easy in theory, difficult in practice…but not for infants. A newly born infant enters the world yearning and rendering love to all who enter the baby's realm. Prior to the onset of influence and knowledge, love is natural; love is inherent with our being. Hate is acquired.

Reciprocal love requires among other things, trust, respect, integrity, and vulnerability. Few people possess the courage of insight and the integrity to recognize, let alone share vulnerability. Fewer still, have the security of being, capacity for understanding and forgiveness, not to take advantage of others by leveraging vulnerability for political/emotional/material advantage. The saying "If you love me, you'll…. (fill in the blank), is the vilest form of manipulation. Leveraging the vulnerability of love or the insecurity of a particular relationship with the fulcrum of emotional extortion debases the challenger not the challenged. Those who would compromise or leverage love for material gain or emotional dominance are unworthy of genuine love. One may respond to that comment with the words, "If you love me, you won't try to unreasonably use love as a bargaining chip, however that reduces one to the level of the manipulator and it is more prudent to walk away and realize that better choices can be made rather than remain in dialog with an emotional vampire. Khalil Gibran said it far better than I, "If you love somebody, let them go, for if they return, they were always yours. And if they don't, they never were."

"Love is patient: love is kind; love is not envious or boastful or arrogant or rude. It does not insist on its own way; it is not irritable or resentful; it does not rejoice in wrongdoing, but rejoices in the truth. It bears all things, believes in all things, hopes all things, endures all things. Love never ends." – 1 Corinthians 13:4-7. Is that not a definition of God?

Love, at it's most sublime, is when we care for another person, and in expressing love, ask nothing in return, acknowledging that to experience love is its own greatest reward. Consider this beautiful passage from the Lebanese poet, Kahlil Gibran:

"Once a man sat at my board and ate my bread and drank my wine,
And went away laughing at me.
Then he came again for bread and wine, and I spurned him;
And the angels laughed at me."

The heart of the calloused man may never change, yet if we too submit to those same calluses, we are self-condemned to a world of shadow. Mankind will remain in a whirlpool of despair if we do not redevelop the courage and strength to love and understand one another, rather than submit to the expedience of ignorance and the weakness of physical aggression. A bumper sticker slogan says, "My kid can beat up your honor student." That may be so, however the people who display those stickers never were or ever could have been honor students. Nathaniel Hawthorne was certainly more eloquent than 21st century bumper-sticker wisdom when he said, "Caresses, expressions of one sort or another, are necessary to the life of the affections as leaves are to the life of a tree. If they are wholly restrained, love will die at the roots."

To love one's self is to have courage to admit vulnerability. To love one's self is to use courage for understanding and nurturing, not domination. Self-love begins with self-acceptance and once that huge step is consummated, one can then love others as ourselves. So many relationships falter because *other* people are expected to fill voids in *our* lives. We then chastise or hold them accountable for *our* faults, which *they* don't "fix". If we cannot trust the actions and integrity of our own lives, how can we expect other people to trust us or treat us with integrity? The truest language of love is expressed with the veracity of virtue and ethic in word and deed.

A story is told of a middle-aged couple that had recently met, each of whom had been divorced. They felt an immediate attraction to each other and as weeks went by, the lady in the relationship wanted to know of the man's intentions. She basically asked, "I love you and I know you love me, but how do I know you won't cheat on me?" The man, who was quite in love with the woman, realized the gravity of the question and told her he would give her an answer when he knew the right words. They were both well educated and both had knowledge beyond their schooling. And the man knew that divorce courts are filled with men who said to their lovers, "There will never be anybody else, I love you so much." After one week, on one of their dates, the man told her, "I have an answer for your question." She asked, "What is it?" He looked directly into her eyes and told her, "I do love you but I also know that many men (and women) have said and meant those words and yet they still had affairs. So I will tell you why this time is different. When I take a vow, any vow for that matter, it is not because I love you that I will keep my vow; it is because I love and honor myself that I will keep my vow. Because I honor myself, and because I choose to extend that fidelity to you with a vow, I will not break my vow." They were married several months later and because of shared vulnerabilities, honor and trust their marriage is greater than the sum of the parts.

Love is not one particular entity. Love is an atom containing a nucleus of integrity, respect, trust, vulnerability, dignity, honor and freedom. When atoms (people) meet, the molecule that forms is the chemistry of the miracle of fulfilling mutual love. The divine aspect of the chemistry of love yields an equation between two people that renders a quotient greater than itself. Many have heard the phrase "love hurts". If that is so, the pleasure-pain anodes of one's emotional battery are crossed. Love is enriching and fulfilling. The only instance love may hurt is through absence. "Absence diminishes mediocre passions and increases the great ones, as the wind extinguishes candles and fans fires." – Rochefoucauld. Is it better to have loved and lost, than never to have loved at all? To have experienced love, and love lost, one may choose to remember the ambrosia of the cup at its fullest or the loss of the ambrosia. Remembering and being present with the loss of love can be a tendency, however in so doing one elects to realize a memory of loss as opposed to a memory of richness; the emptiness of the cup rather than rejoicing in the fullness of the immortality of love. "Thousands of candles can be lighted from a single candle, and the life of the candle will not be shortened. Happiness never decreases by being shared" – Buddha.

Quite simply, pain and suffering is negative; nurturing and understanding are positive. Physical or emotional slavery to a person or doctrine, not of one's choosing, is detrimental; freedom is beneficial. The Marquis de Sade might as well have written any gospel not attuned to the proper orientation of pleasure/pain. The definition of the Catholic doctrine of transubstantiation, which concerns *what* is changed, not *how* the change occurs, is given in the following words of the thirteenth session of the Council of Trent, quoted in paragraph 1376 of the Catechism of the Catholic Church: "Because Christ our Redeemer said that it was truly his body that he was offering under the species of bread, it has always been the conviction of the Church of God, and this holy Council now declares again, that by the consecration of the bread and wine there takes place a change of the whole substance of the bread into the substance of the body of Christ our Lord and of the whole substance of the wine into the substance of his blood. This change the holy Catholic Church has fittingly and properly called transubstantiation." Through revelation or psychological projection, the Catholic Church has determined a vehicle with which to equate the body of its Savior with bread and the blood of its Savior with wine. One wonders how the clever minds of centuries past originated and subsequently perpetuated the equivocation of sacrament with cannibalism. One does not need a degree from a seminary to consider there are better ways to pay homage to our Creator than by *drinking His blood and eating His body!* Yet, force of habit (a lie told often enough can beg belief) prohibits practicing Catholics from acknowledging this horrendous ceremony. Transubstantiation would seem to be the doctrinal term for vampirism and cannibalism, as applied to divine worship, scripture by the Marquis de Sade.

Freedom is best expressed when eschewing the bonds of miasmic religious doctrine. Freedom consists of two parts, the ability to be free to do something and the freedom not to do something. Freedom of speech is universally acknowledged to be integral to the fabric of any free society. More significantly however it is far less universally understood that freedom also means the choice not to participate in the unwholesome emotions and insecurities of people who have contaminated motives or less than honorable intentions. "Sticks and stones will break my bones, but names will never hurt me." As children we try to bear that adage in mind to minimize the effect of immature behavior of our peers. As adults we totally forget what we learned as children. Emotional freedom is surrendered when one voluntarily submits to the immaturity, insecurity, or slander of emotional vampires who feed the ego by preying on victims they eagerly seek. Emotional vampirism can manifest in either of two forms, personal or institutional. Personal vampirism involves the emotional extortion of a person vis-à-vis another person or group of people, i.e. "If you love me...you'll do what I want." Institutionalized vampirism exists when extortion comes in the form of salvation/ damnation in the realm of religion or ideology in the realm of politics.

People are most apt to surrender emotional freedom when threatened by fear. Freedom recedes in direct proportion to fear. Overwhelming physical force by weapon or fist can produce fear of bodily harm. Overwhelming emotional force and intimidation can cause spiritual despair. Overwhelming spiritual despair...Christian doctrine teaches that God sent his only begotten Son to die for our sins. What type of father would consign to abet progenicide, the death of his son or daughter? In any context, only a deranged person of criminal mind would be guilty of such a crime. When Christianity expounds a doctrine that "God so loved the world that he gave (sacrificed) His only begotten Son" it serves to reinforce the dysfunction of mankind's pleasure/pain impulse referred to above.

Overwhelming spiritual harm; the Genesis account of Abraham and Isaac that mirrors the courtship of death. Genesis 22:1-2, "After these things God tested Abraham, and said to him, "Abraham!" And he said, "Here am I." He said, "Take your son, your only son Isaac, whom you love, and go to the land of Moriah, and offer him there as a burnt offering upon one of the mountains of which I shall tell you." Proceeding to Genesis 22:11-12, "But the angel of the LORD called to him from heaven, and said, "Abraham, Abraham!" And he said, "Here am I." He said, "Do not lay your hand on the lad or do anything to him; for now I know that you fear God, seeing you have not withheld your son, your only son, from me."

Among the juris law of man exists the Geneva Convention, which prohibits military combatants from physical and emotional torture of other combatants. God however, being all-powerful, deserves a pass and may resort to mentally bludgeoning mind-games and blood sacrifice. What kind of God could be so emotionally barbaric? Perhaps as significantly, because God is not barbaric, what kind of people would represent God in this way, and for what reason? Apologists argue that God would not sanction human sacrifice, that this exercise was necessary to test Abraham's faith. In this way, the New Century Version of Genesis changes verse 12 of Genesis to "I know that you trust God" (deleting fear and inserting trust). However in either blasphemous case, *fear* of God or *trust* of God has nothing to do with *faith* in God. These passages have nothing to do with faith. What type of faith would excuse *any* type of manipulation or sacrifice (bloodlust), animal or human? And what type of apologist, in so doing, would try to qualify such behavior? The actions of apologists such as these are similar to attorneys who prevent the conviction of a murderer due to a technicality in legal procedure.

The episode of Abraham and Isaac deals with suppression, obedience, and fear to the point where a father would unquestioningly murder his beloved only begotten son! And apparently doing so without the knowledge or consent of his wife Sarah! Further observations would include the point that such fear and manipulation from God would necessarily set an example for those who vouchsafe that same fear. This endemic fear *fostered by divinity* would seemingly hold believers unaccountable for similar intimidations and manipulations presented under the guise of doctrine and belief. Further, please consider that sacrifice is voluntary not mandatory. Voluntary sacrifice is giving alms. Mandatory sacrifice is extortion whether taking money, or more significantly, freedom of spirit. Lastly, Genesis 22:13 speaks of Abraham sacrificing a ram. How can anyone assume to believe that God would exalt in the needless death of any creature. Examples of the wrath of God/Allah in religious text serve solely to perpetuate without question or qualification the insecurities and paranoia ingrained in canonized text.

Toxic behavior by people (predators) who prey or dominate (a subliminal effort to elicit sacrifice), whether or not inspired by canonized text, manifest his or her own insecurity, not the perceived insecurities of those to whom the behavior is being directed. Though living several generations apart and having an ocean between them, Thomas Paine shared at least one viewpoint with Friedrich Nietzsche when he commented, "Belief in a cruel God makes a cruel man."

A worried Jesuit once reckoned that "the hymns of Luther killed [converted] more souls than his sermons." Conversely, one might wish to consider that quite possibly, canonized religious text of missionary religions has anesthetized our spirits; has killed the same souls to whom the Jesuit referred. Quoting Spanish philosopher George Santayana (1863-1952), *Soliloquies in England,* "My atheism, like that of Spinoza, is true piety towards the universe and denies only gods fashioned by men in their own image, to be servants of their human interests." The veracity of Santayana's statement lays waste to the belief in, and apologies for, the wrath of God/Allah. The imaginary wrath of God is suffered (and thus the [pre]dominance of religion persists) because, and only because, of promised riches that abound in Heaven. If the motive behind a good deed is material reward (all types of precious stones) that which matters is not the goodness of the deed, so much as the reward. Karmic law would indicate that no karmic positives are accrued in material-based reward because emotionally the effect of goodness was neutralized by the reward. The deed is incidental because the motivating factor is the reward. Religious shepherds regard their "flock" in much the same way we domesticate our pets with the reward of a treat when they "learn" to perform a conditioned response.

Verily, means do not justify ends, and in compliment, ends do not justify means. Consider that in the dimension of time, "end" is a non-existent concept, consequently, all that matters is the means, i.e. the honor, dignity, and integrity we implement to govern our thoughts, words, and actions. Spiritus mundi has suffered the burden of original sin and the polarity of reward/threat, justification/recrimination of heaven/hell of religious dogma for two millennia and is steeped more than ever in violence, terror, famine, and…samodaya.

The promise of ultimate heavenly reward creates a flat and arid spiritual horizon for spiritus mundi with regard to future incarnations. This would seem to indicate cause-and-effect as to why spiritus mundi continues to witness increasing violence, conflict, and emptiness (samodaya). As witnessed by the condition of humanity in the 2007 years since the life of Christ, arguably we have made virtually no spiritual progress. Considering Karmic Law, the promise of heavenly reward acts much the same as a spiritual negative-mortgage. If reward is expected now or forever, a deed is rendered worthless. In an ethos of balance without consideration for "reward", a job well done or a deed of benevolence renders wellness sufficient of itself and is reflected as such within the hearts of those who have done so and the reward is immediate.

"Generosity is giving more than you can and pride is taking less than you need." – Khalil Gibran.

Conduct seeking material reward negates altruism. When based on materialism, conduct diminishes in direct proportion to diminishing rewards. The converse may also be true whereby behavior becomes dependent on rewards of increasing value, much the same as an addict needing a higher fix. Ask a sales executive whether or not threats and incentives influence sales. A parent may capitulate to the emotional extortion of a young child or teen by offering reward and then escalating rewards to appease them into compliance. When the escalation of reward is no longer effective, the next tactic is generally (for one or both parties) anger and/or the mirror image of reward; threat. Threat becomes reward if threat is not enacted. Parents and executives in these scenarios lack the discipline not to offer reward and are thus mired in relationships that are based on the tension and stress of threat/reward rather than altruism and discipline. Threat/reward is no different in religion. Ask a priest about the marketing effectiveness of the threat of damnation in hell or the reward of heavenly delight.

The Greek philosopher Plato lived in the mid-to-late fourth century. He was the most famous of Socrates' pupils who carried on much of his former teacher's work and eventually in 385 A. D. founded his own school, the Academy that would become in its time, the most famous school in the classical world. For Plato, human beings exist in a duality composed of visible and intelligible things. The visible world is what surrounds us: what we see, what we hear, what we experience, given that the visible world exists amid constant change. The other part of existence is the intelligible world made up of the unchanging products of human reason: anything arising from reason alone, such as abstract definitions or mathematics (noumenon) makes up this intelligible world, which is the world of thought. The intelligible world consists of eternal "**forms**", (from the Greek, *idea)* of things; the visible world is the imperfect and changing manifestation in this world of these unchanging forms (phenomenon). For example, the "Form" or "Idea" of a bird is intelligible, abstract, and applies to all birds; the concept of "bird" remains constant though species of birds proliferate among themselves—the "form" of a bird would never change even if every bird became extinct. The life force of an individual bird is expressed in a physical, changing object that ceases to exist as a bird until the transition of death however, the "form" or "idea" of a bird, or "birdness" does not change. As a physical object, a bird only makes sense in that it can be referred to the "Form" or "Idea" of avian existence. Phenomenon dictates that a human being has four limbs. When a limb is lost, the limb no longer exists in reality (Phenomenon) however it does exist essentially (noumenon). This explains why amputees genuinely feel limbs they have lost. Noumenon, in the classic philosophical sense, may describe the condition of awareness amidst eternity.

Only the progression of time determines the distinction between elements that exist within the dynamic realms of reality and imagination. All the elements of civilization originate from the imagination of Homo Divinitas id est his Divine ability to create ideas (images). Homo Divinitas then determines and invents means of production to create (make real, realize) his pragmatic environment (affairs, occurrences) and spiritual expression, id est art and worship.

The world in which we live, the condition of man, spiritus mundi fraught with deception piled upon myth and dupery, is presently replicated in most of society as a replication of the Mad-hatter's tea party from Lewis Carroll's masterpiece, *Alice's Adventures in Wonderland*, which may have been a masterpiece of Platonic philosophy. Everything real is imaginary, and everything imaginary is real. Spirituality has been seduced by "religion" because religion promises a heaven defined by and fraught with Materialism, the subsequent value of material, and the desire to enjoy and accumulate material wealth of value and abundance.

Behavior is governed by the lowest common denominator when reduced to, and equated with material reward. When spiritual wellness is fostered on the basis of the reward of paradise (heaven) we are no less than unwitting prostitutes who barter good behavior for reward. Spiritual casting couches are sponsored by the Vatican, Mecca, anywhere the concubine (believer) trades works of integrity for a heaven fraught with riches denied on earth. The authors of gospel text of any religion do the afterlife a disservice if the best they can do is portray heaven by pandering to vanity (outward beauty), greed (all manner of precious stones and gold), and sexual gratification (promiscuity, as with the virgins of Islamic Jannat). Eight hundred years prior to Plato, the Roman philosopher Democritus defined a viewpoint conducive to happiness in this world or the next, "Men find happiness neither by means of the body or possessions, but through uprightness and wisdom." Democritus was not merely a philosopher; he was a pioneer in mathematics in general and geometry in particular. He remarked of his passion for geometry (and his loathing of power), "I would rather discover a single cause than become king of the Persians." Wisdom deigns power, insecurity lusts for power.

Vatican pronouncements that are issued "ex cathedra" mean they are issued as "from the throne". As advocated in *A New Reformation*, in heaven, the beggar is no different than a prince, an emerald no more valuable than a pebble. It should be said that a throne is no different than a chair. Beggar and prince, pebble and emerald, chair and throne, all imply value in relation to each other. *Rosebud* theorizes that heaven represents the antithesis not the epitome of value. Hence, the evidence of the crime to which Arthur C. Clark refers, "The greatest tragedy in mankind's entire history may be the hijacking of morality by religion."

Good works remain not so much because of, but in spite of those who insist on and believe in a wrathful God, intent on the orgy of violence upon judgment day, final or otherwise. The Qu'ran, Book of Revelation, Book of Hebrews all speak of vengeance. The present spiritus mundi of Homo Divinitas is one that reflects the selfsame violence, conflict, and emotional oppression of the New Testament, the Old Testament, and the Qu'ran of Islam. This is not to say there is not conflict and violence in India, China, and other countries of the east, yet how much of the violence of spiritus mundi is the result of reaction, not action. Much as innocent children, society when in infancy, accepted the "revelations of the anointed" under the threat of eternal hell if they did not. Hell exists solely in the minds of those who propagandize hell. Organized religion benefits from the myth of sin thus perpetuating a mindset of domination and salvation. The selfishness of domination craves emotional fealty and sacrifice; the benevolence of giving enables charity. Domination is the antithesis of freedom.

Just as freedom retreats in direct proportion to fear, fear cowers in direct proportion to courage. Freedom of spiritual expression necessitates courage such as when facing a bully in a dark alley. The dark alley and the "dark ages" may seem as euphemism, however no less accurately so. Leaving the dark alley of doctrine involves developing the initiative to seek, and the determination to find, answers in philosophies of thought, reason, and yes, faith. A spirit enjoying the freedom of flight is ever so much more beautiful than the pathos of the caged bird. Though, it must be mentioned too, that freedom has so much more meaning having experienced the cage. Therein lies the duality of existence.

Part of the dialectic of discerning the duality of being, the decision-making process, is the assimilation of fact, periodically accompanied by certain assumptions. Facts and assumptions accompanied with considerations to moral and ethical principles will render any decision, as it should be, without regard to the result. It is not whether you win or lose, rather how you play the came that matters. When ethics and morality guide the decision-making process the result is True, regardless of the relative perception of the outcome being "good" or "bad". The weak of spirit will pounce like a hyena on those persons whose decisions have seemingly, at least for the time being, turned out "wrongly". This is most often done by saying, "*assume*, means you have made an *ass* of *u* and *me*." Incidentally, that verbal broadside has nothing to do with *their* concern for *your* welfare. And further, one never hears of the hundreds of assumptions that are correct. People are indignant at their own inconvenience and don't have the emotional maturity to accept the consequence of the situation. It is always easy to blame and more difficult to solve. Blame is an emotional slingshot used by the insecure to attempt to bring someone else down to his or her level. Have the freedom *not* to accept their "gift" of pettiness. Realize the behavior of the weak of spirit for what it is and refuse to participate in their insecurity. The weak of spirit will seldom have the courage to acknowledge an opportunity for learning and spiritual growth because in so doing, they would necessarily need to admit that the other party in the endeavor in which they are involved is "better". The spiritually weak will always choose to reduce someone else to their level rather than have the courage to acknowledge the opportunity to rise to their level.

The same high level of self-esteem will realize criticism for what it is. More often than not, when evaluating any given situation, one person may say of the other, "You're too ...fill in the blank". For instance, you're going too fast, or you're going too slow, or...ad infinitum. The covert part of any sentence that begins such as these, ends with the words: *for me...(my ego)*. What the other person is saying is an evaluation of your actions in relation to their opinions. Their assumption is that *their* opinions are always the best gauge if not the perfect gauge for *your* life.

There is a phrase, "It's more foolish to argue with a fool than to be one." The foolhardy are such because they do not have the emotional or intellectual courage to admit difference or error. Beyond error, vis-à-vis the relationship between "right" and "wrong", it is significant to acknowledge the freedom to be gained by realizing the nature of decision-making. No one of sound mind ever knowingly, purposefully, or intentionally makes "wrong" decisions. "Good" decisions may be made that turn out "badly" or vice versa. However the outcome of decisions are egoic interpretations of them and those interpretations and/or perceptions can change with the passage of time. It would consequently follow that freedom from consequence (guilt on one hand or pride on the other) occurs when, in anticipating any particular circumstance, decisions are made with the greatest attention to honesty, integrity, and honor, thus permitting actions to take their due and True course.

Post-event criticisms do exist and can be appropriate when offered constructively. However, comments made destructively are merely another form of complaint, which indicate the insecurity of the accuser more than the veracity of the accused. Differences in viewpoints are probably apparent to the participants involved. Concepts are accurate or inaccurate, factual or not factual however rarely is there reason to take refuge in being "right" other than the insecure impulse of making the other person "wrong". Seldom do "right" and "wrong" exist, yet for the most part; the weak and insecure ego will always seek the moral "high" ground of righteousness.

CHAPTER 11
THE MYSTERY

"Do not believe in anything simply because it is found written in your religious books. Do not believe in anything merely on the authority of your teachers and elders. Do not believe in traditions because they have been handed down for many generations. But after observation and analysis, when you find that anything agrees with reason and is conducive to the good and benefit of one and all, then accept it and live up to it."
– Buddha.

Speaking of the 19th century philosopher Friedrich Nietzsche (1844-1900) Karen Armstrong states, "Nietzsche realized that there had been a radical shift in the consciousness of the West which would make it increasingly difficult to believe in the phenomenon most people described as "God". Not only had our science made such notions as the literal understanding of creation an impossibility, but our greater control and power made the idea of a divine overseer unacceptable."[39] Speaking of one of Nietzsche's contemporaries, Ms. Armstrong continues, "Sigmund Freud (1856-1939) certainly regarded belief in God as an illusion that mature men and women should lay aside. The idea of God was not a lie but a device of the unconscious, which needed to be decoded by psychology. A personal god was nothing more than an exalted father figure: desire for such a deity sprang from infantile yearnings for a powerful protective father, for justice and fairness and for life to go on forever. God is simply a projection of these desires, feared and worshipped by human beings out of an abiding sense of helplessness. Religion belonged to the infancy of the human race; it had been a necessary stage in the transition from childhood to maturity. It had promoted ethical values which were essential to society. Now that humanity had come of age, however, it should be left behind."[40] The helplessness of mankind to which Ms. Armstrong alludes begs the age-old creationist question, which came first, the chicken or the egg, organized religion or helplessness, helplessness or organized religion?

No one can assume to know the private motivations of any individual. Herr Freud was a powerful intellect, instrumental in establishing the psychoanalytic school of psychology. Bearing this in mind. Would a cobbler not mend a shoe or for that matter, a cooper, a barrel? Is Freud no different from Augustine who formulated the doctrine of Original Sin to create a need for salvation? Freud's discipline of psychoanalysis brings to mind a quote from the German philosopher Johann Gottlieb Fichte who died 42 years before Freud was born. Fichte said, "What sort of philosophy one chooses depends on what sort of person one is." Freud's school of thought was his philosophy and thus, may have erroneously influenced the interpretation of man's perception of the psyche just as "original sin" was a religious misinterpretation applied to the spirit of mankind.

John McKay left the University of Southern California in 1976 to become the first head coach of the Tampa Bay Buccaneers of the National Football League. In one of his earliest press conferences Coach McKay mentioned he had a 5-year plan to take the expansion Buccaneers to the Super Bowl. When a sports journalist asked the coach why he had a 5-year plan, coach McKay replied (perhaps facetiously!) that he had a 5-year contract. Coach McKay was a glib and gifted man with a dry wit. It is one thing to guide a football team to success with one's own particular expertise and agenda it is quite another matter indeed to influence the minds of generations of people with psycho-hypothesis (Freud), deicide (Nietzsche), or original sin (Augustine).

The point of the anecdotes above is that to find God/Allah/The Great Integrity, perhaps we need to look no farther than the closest mirror. Certainly, if nothing else, the reflection will render a physical image of a Divine creation. To the academy of sciences that demand proof of Divinity, none will be forthcoming. Proof would provide answers and deny Homo Divinitas of the mystery of the journey, and the circumstances therein, toward Truth and fulfillment. At least for now, in the dimensions we currently experience, the point of the exercise is to enjoy and learn amidst the mystery during the journey. The destination, which is to say our destiny, will take care of itself. Destiny (transition) will be upon each person as a thief in the night. Only then will answers and *proof* be apparent. The Angel of Death may call at any moment. It is our choice whether or not to honor each day and each person in it or take them for granted and let them pass as grains through the hourglass, realizing, *after its too late,* that we wish once again to have one more precious day to live. Just once again to re-experience those precious moments just one more time. Realize each day, as it's own blessing because tomorrow never arrives. Today, once gone, is irretrievable. We may choose to realize that Divinity is dead or we may not. If however, we carefully listen amidst silence, visualize with the mind's eye instead of ocular vision, and feel with our hearts as well as our senses, we are able to realize that Divinity is not dead. Divinity is alive in this reader and this author. Homo Divinitas is aware of Deity not because of knowledge per se, but rather because of affection in his heart. Our perception of Deity must be reconstituted from one of wrath and power to one of love and understanding. If we no longer emulate the power and wrath of the Deity as portrayed in the scriptures of Islam and Christianity, perhaps the power of love will supplant the love of power.

No universal correct answers exist in response to the questions of the mystery of the journey or to the mystery of the destination. Each individual is on a unique journey of destiny to find accurate answers that lead toward enlightenment, heaven or nirvana. The roadblocks of doctrine, bigotry, or fear should not impede the journey. Book burners of Nazi-Germany attempted to inhibit freedom of opinion, belief, and thought. Political dogmatists in government and religion endeavor to intimidate and dominate the free flow of ideas and philosophies. Book burners in the 1930's were rather primitive in their efforts to censor thought. They straightforwardly and unabashedly burned books.

Censorship of a more sophisticated albeit more sinister form presents itself in the form of "heresy". In the realm of theological discourse, the charge of heresy does not require kerosene yet it accomplishes the same objective when levied against those in pursuit of spiritual wholeness. Revisiting Tertullian once again, the Catholic Encyclopedia extols how Tertullian dealt with heresy and heretics, "Two or three years later (about 200) Tertullian assaulted heresy in a treatise even more brilliant, which, unlike the *"Apologeticus"*, is not for his own day only but for all time. It is called *"Liber de Praescriptione Haereticorum"*. Prescription now means the right obtained to something by long usage. In Roman law the signification was wider; it meant the cutting short of a question by the refusal to hear the adversary's arguments, on the ground of an anterior point which must cut away the ground under his feet. So Tertullian deals with heresies: it is of no use to listen to their arguments or refute them, for we have a number of antecedent proofs that they cannot deserve a hearing. Heresies, he begins, must not astonish us, for they were prophesied. Heretics urge the text, "Seek and ye shall find", but this was not said to Christians; we have a rule of faith to be accepted without question. "Let curiosity give place to faith and vain glory make way for salvation", so Tertullian parodies a line of Cicero's.[41]

In other words, repetition makes right. Tertullian could not have Cicero excommunicated because Cicero was a philosopher not a Catholic, but that did not stop Tertullian from making an effort to mock Cicero. Cicero has been a reknowned Roman philosopher for many years, but he was only one of many disdained by Tertullian to wit, "We should then be never required to try our strength in contests about the soul with **philosophers, those patriarchs of heretics**, as they may be fairly called. The apostle (Paul), so far back as his own time, foresaw, indeed, that **philosophy would do violent injury to the truth**" (De anima, 3).[42] Don't ask, don't read, don't question. German poet Heinrich Heine (1797-1856) could not have foreseen the Salem (Massachusetts) Witch Trials one hundred years prior to his birth. Whether he did or not, his insight and "prophesy" is remarkable, "Where they have burned books, they will end in burning human beings."

A repertoire of too many books or too many ideas never obscures the path of enlightenment. Though to be sure, the most insidious condition to plague mankind is not necessarily the control of thought-police so much as the sloth of apathy. A book not read, a poem not experienced, passively serves the same purpose as kerosene. In either case, if the book is not read, wisdom is not gleaned from our forbears and for all practical purposes, does not exist. Contrary to the ignorance of book burning, one may consider that book reading may light a candle of curiosity, and it is better to light a candle than curse the darkness.

Ray Bradbury who, in 2004, was presented with the National Medal of Arts Award by George and Laura Bush wrote a science-fiction novel entitled, *Fahrenheit 451*. Mr. Bradbury based the title of his book on the theoretical temperature at which a book begins to burn. The premise of *Fahrenheit 451* is that mankind will determine a way to defeat ideological totalitarians even if they must become the books themselves…by immortalizing the books through memorization. In a less devout way, we are influenced by, learn, and adopt, thought, wisdom, and philosophies that have been gifted to us by the wisest of our forefathers. If we do not avail ourselves of our heritage of ideas, knowledge, thought, theory, and wisdom, we will stagnate as sure as a plant without water.

The attempt must be made to pass the baton of gnosis to succeeding generations and to search for new ideas of the mind and understandings of the heart. The fertile garden of knowledge and philosophy are present in literature to be enjoyed by the mind as surely as the bounty of food exists for the supper table. Nazis banned books, and religion portrays knowledge as original sin. Some may wish to give Saint Augustine the benefit of doubt regarding his motivations in formulating the doctrine of "original sin", because intelligent men can differ. Further, men of maturity can agree to disagree. Still, one must assert that Augustine's intentions were less than wholesome when he insisted that Pelagius *and his followers* be deemed heretical following the Synod of Hippo.

Augustine's "defense" however would be that he was only following orders. One of many examples in the Bible of random, callous, and senseless persecution can be found in Revelation 2:20-23, "Notwithstanding I have a few things against thee, because thou sufferest that woman Jezebel, which calleth herself a prophetess, to teach and to seduce my servants to commit fornication, and to eat things sacrificed unto idols. And I gave her space to repent of her fornication; and she repented not. Behold, I will cast her into a bed, and them that commit adultery with her into great tribulation, except they repent of their deeds. And I will kill her children with death; and all the churches shall know that I am he which searcheth the reins and hearts: and I will give unto every one of you according to your works. I WILL KILL HER CHILDREN? Little difference exists between the Bible and Qu'ran. Quoting Surah 3:10-12, "(As for) those who disbelieve, surely neither their wealth nor their children shall avail them in the least against Allah, and these it is who are the fuel of the fire. Like the striving of the people of Firon and those before them; they rejected our communications, so Allah destroyed them on account of their faults; and Allah is severe in requiting (evil). Say to those who disbelieve: You shall be vanquished, and driven together to hell; and evil is the resting-place." Vanity, vengeance, and vindictiveness…who were these people who portrayed our Creator in such a way?

Vanity, vengeance, and vindictiveness continue in the book of Deuteronomy, verses 1-9, "If there arise among you a prophet, or a dreamer of dreams, and giveth thee a sign or a wonder, And the sign or the wonder come to pass, whereof he spake unto thee, saying,

Let us go after other gods, which thou hast not known, and let us serve them; Thou shalt not hearken unto the words of that prophet, or that dreamer of dreams: for the LORD your God proveth you, to know whether ye love the LORD your God with all your heart and with all your soul. Ye shall walk after the LORD your God, and fear him, and keep his commandments, and obey his voice, and ye shall serve him, and cleave unto him. And that prophet, or that dreamer of dreams, shall be put to death; because he hath spoken to turn you away from the LORD your God, which brought you out of the land of Egypt, and redeemed you out of the house of bondage, to thrust thee out of the way which the LORD thy God commanded thee to walk in. So shalt thou put the evil away from the midst of thee. If thy brother, the son of thy mother, or thy son, or thy daughter, or the wife of thy bosom, or thy friend, which is as thine own soul, entice thee secretly, saying, Let us go and serve other gods, which thou hast not known, thou, nor thy fathers; Namely, of the gods of the people which are round about you, nigh unto thee, or far off from thee, from the one end of the earth even unto the other end of the earth; Thou shalt not consent unto him, nor hearken unto him; neither shall thine eye pity him, neither shalt thou spare, neither shalt thou conceal him: But thou shalt surely kill him; thine hand shall be first upon him to put him to death, and afterwards the hand of all the people."

Again quoting from *I Am My Best Self*, "Black white rich poor; we are all from the One Source. The same Power that directs the movements of the planets and the changing seasons flows through all of us. We are all connected. What we give out to the world, will come back to us...for there is nowhere else to go! When next you admire the boundless beauty and generosity of nature, know that this too is how you really are. Listen to your Best Self and you will hear it say: We are all one."

"For books are not absolutely dead things, but…do preserve as in a vial the purest efficacy and extraction of that living intellect that bred them. I know they are as lively, and as vigorously productive, as those fabulous Dragon's teeth; and being sown up and down, may chance to spring up armed men. And yet on the other hand unless warriors be used as good almost kill a man as a good Book; who kills a man kills a reasonable creature, God's image; but he who destroys a good book, kills Reason itself, kills the Image of God, as it were in the eye. Many a man lives a burden to the Earth; but a good book is the precious life-blood of a master-spirit, embalmed and treasured upon purpose to a life beyond life." – John Milton, *Areopagitica*. John Milton was a genius. It does not take a genius to understand there is more divine spirituality in Dipa De Motwane's *I Am My Best Self* than the book of Deuteronomy.

"Never doubt that a small group of thoughtful committed citizens can change the world; indeed, it's the only thing that ever has." – Margaret Mead.

A Doctorate of Divinity or degrees in theology are measures of education in the field of religion. Learned people who possess such credentials are to be applauded. They should not however be misconstrued as being "in on" the inside track to salvation. Nor should clergy be confused with those of Messianic tendencies who consider themselves "anointed" with spiritual omnipotence such as those who claim to have conversations with God. People who truly wish to emulate God can best do so not necessarily by reading religious text so much as heeding his or her own conscience. "Conscience!

Conscience! Divine instinct, immortal voice from heaven; sure guide of a creature ignorant and finite indeed, yet intelligent and free, infallible, judge of good and evil, making man like to God!" – Jean-Jacques Rousseau (1712-1778). Conscience leads us to the Greater Law of Man, of Homo Divinitas. Adherence to moral and ethical absolutes that do not change with the passage of time, and living an existence emulating those absolutes, represents the most difficult, yet most rewarding journey of all.

For two millennia, the Christian religion has acknowledged that decisions made during the journey of life are made amidst a condition of "free will". "Free will" was mentioned three times in previous chapters. This, as in many other doctrinal issues, is not etymologically accurate. Because words are very powerful, words need to be used accurately, thus the following clarification. The soul of Homo Divinitas expresses choice of mind and heart in a condition of "free thought" or "free intent" that is subject to ratification of Deity, which is to say, karmic law. Homo sapiens cannot "will" something to happen though his or her ego may convince them they have the "power" to do so. All people have tried to exert willpower to make something happen to no avail. This is so because it was not destined (permitted) to happen because karmic law (*God's will*) has determined otherwise. Action, cause, and result are determined to occur in harmony with the greater issue of karmic destiny (we reap as we sow) as opposed to personal desire. Therefore, each of us may deign the call of egoic selfishness and give credence to the clarion (trumpet) call of conscience. "We must become the change we wish to see in the world." – Mahatma Gandhi. When Homo Divinitas exercises the wisdom to pursue conscience and wisdom in lieu of expedience and selfishness the world can be changed to a *spiritus mundi* of brotherhood. Incumbent on Homo Divinitas is to self-canonize his or her own bible. "Make your own bible. Select and collect all the words and sentences that in all your readings have been to you like the blast of a trumpet", a blast of the trumpet sounding the fanfare of dignity, honor, Truth, and integrity of the *un*common man. LIVE THEM, BELIEVE THEM, IMMORTALIZE THEM, follow the trumpet, **be** the blast of the trumpet, **be** a spiritual sovereign (summa cum spiritus), **be** Homo Divinitas.

EPILOGUE

This work has attempted to apply a deep-tissue massage for people in need of reinforcement of spirit. Virtually all persons, through the course of their lives are faced with daunting challenges and heartbreak. All people too, experience happiness and elation. I have tried, in my own way, to communicate that hardship is best dealt with through honor, and abundance with humility. John Paul Moore wrote a tender yet compelling poem entitled, *I'm Drinking From The Saucer*, in which he says:

May I never be too busy
To help bear another's load;
I'm drinking from the saucer
'Cause my cup has overflowed.

The perfect beauty of the symphony of Homo Divinitas may be expressed with the clarion call of the trumpet or the whisper of the flute. Each instrument, each person, has beauty, each in his or her own way. We, each, are a singular unique universe, fully responsible for who we are, what we do, and how we create and harvest ourselves amidst the miracle of the different facets of incarnation. To the extent we blame others, to the extent we lack the impetus of self-direction under the moral compass of conscience, to the extent we do not possess ourselves with a rudder of self-reliance and self-esteem, we are self-condemned to the doldrums of spiritual mediocrity and/or the anesthesia of apathy, or worse, self-loathing. Have the courage to try, have the courage to seek. Failure is a temporary condition that precedes achievement. Benjamin Franklin once commented, "Genius without education is like silver in the mine." Genius will not necessarily lead to happiness, but mining will! In that same vein (sic), Mr. Franklin also said, "Having been poor is no shame, but being ashamed of it is."

A corollary to Mr. Franklin's statement would follow that there should be shame when material wealth is gained by spiritual compromise. If someone is so blessed as to be able to say, "In my own life, there is no one else I would rather be, and there is nothing in or about my life I would change", such is a profoundly happy individual. This author is such an individual. I accept pain as I accept joy. I accept disappointment because in so doing, satisfaction has greater dimension. And, if merely for practical purposes in meeting life's challenges, echoing Nietzsche with a twist…adversity met with courage and ethic make me stronger while felicity and fortune met with humility and grace make me stronger still. As I accept and participate in joy, I am reminded of Lewis Carroll, "While the laughter of joy is in full harmony with our deeper life, the laughter of amusement should be kept apart from it. The danger is too great of thus learning to look at solemn things in a spirit of mockery, and to seek in them opportunities for exercising wit."

Far more eloquently than I, Ralph Waldo Emerson defined success as, "To laugh often and much; To win the respect of intelligent people and the affection of children; To earn the appreciation of honest critics and endure the betrayal of false friends; To appreciate beauty, to find the best in others; To leave the world a bit better, whether by a healthy child, a garden patch, or a redeemed social condition; To know even one life has breathed easier because you have lived. This is to have succeeded."

I acknowledge mistakes in order not to repeat them. I forgive others so I am not enchained. I cannot presume to tell anyone what to do or what not to do. I can however, write of my experiences and observations having dealt with tens of thousands of people from all over the planet, having observed and learned from their commonalities and habits, foibles and strengths. First and foremost, I have learned from those experiences and exposures, to love self and honor self with each word and deed. Having crossed that Rubicon, one may enable oneself to love and honor others, and at least, permit them to seek answers to life and beyond in a way of their own choosing. Homo Divinitas is capable of creating miracles. If you do not believe in miracles, witness the adoption of a child; develop the discipline, strength, and courage to face down your worst fear.

Though I consider myself a simple man, my wife is probably more accurate when she says I am a complex man with simple desires. Within eighteen months (October 2005 thru March 2007) I have authored *A New Reformation*, *Rosebud*, and *Toward Spiritual Sovereignty*. I have done so without a college degree and without ever having taken any writing courses. This may be evident in the literary style of the work but not the essence of the work. Nevertheless I have been blessed by the confluence of time, circumstance, determination and discipline, to be able to write these books. The time and circumstance of the equation are elements over which I had no control. That was the easy part. The difficulty was staying the course of my own life experience and in so doing develop the determination and discipline of self-reliance and self-esteem in order to prepare for events I could not have foreseen, authorship being only one of them. "I love those who can smile in trouble, who can gather strength from distress, and grow brave by reflection. 'Tis the business of little minds to shrink, but they whose heart is firm, and whose conscience approves their conduct, will pursue their principles unto death." – Leonardo da Vinci.

Everyone can change the universe for the better by first changing themselves. Should someone choose to emulate the persons quoted herein, may they be blessed on their journey of fulfillment. If not, certainly the journey will provide unique answers for anyone on a path of enlightenment. Within that context, I mention once again the Zen quote of such poetry, "The snow falls, each flake in its appropriate place." The influence of a gentle breeze of empathy and understanding can shape the destiny of the fall of every snowflake, and each one of us has the ability and potential to be the breeze that can shape destiny.

The trilogy of work I have created, *A New Reformation*, *Rosebud*, and *Toward Spiritual Sovereignty* are, in a sense, revolutionary in spirit. Having been born in 1948, I was aware of the extraordinary era during which I came of age. To those of us of similar age, the mid-to-late '60's represented cataclysmic change. The unbridled dreams and idealism of a budding generation on the verge of the Age of Aquarius careened foursquare against those who actively or passively supported the vilest of human endeavor; war. The realities of the political, economical, and military-industrial forces buried our dreams into the ground of Viet Nam. As teens and young adults of the first post-WW2 generation, we had not the voice, opportunity, wisdom or sophistication to change the world. **NOW WE DO**.

Forty years later we are now embroiled in a war in Iraq. A war that was the result of concocted intelligence causing this nation, as *never* before to throw the first punch. Though the coalition troops now engaged in Iraq were not conscripted, their sacrifice is just as profound, their pain is just as real, and the cross-continent disillusionment of the world at large is undeniable and deserved. Untold dreams and idealism are now being buried in the desert sands of Iraq and Afghanistan at the hands of politicians who cloak their power-lust with the oldest trick in the book, the flag of patriotism. "In all history, there is no war which was not hatched by the governments, the governments alone, independent of the interests of the people, to whom war is always pernicious even when successful." – Leo Tolstoy. People, who plead for an end to the war, are called unpatriotic by those not in combat! Once again, quoting Aldous Huxley, "One of the great attractions of patriotism - it fulfills our worst wishes. In the person of our nation we are able, vicariously, to bully and cheat. Bully and cheat, what's more, with a feeling that we are profoundly virtuous." Mr. Huxley once again, "Idealism is the noble toga that political gentlemen drape over their will to power." As with classical thought here again, it would seem "Dubya" is unfamiliar with contemporary thought as well. The best way to support the troops is to bring them home to their families but **MANY PEOPLE REMAIN SILENT**. The silence and helplessness persists and the United States government in confusing stubbornness with courage continues to pledge lives and limbs of coalition members instead of their own!

We of the post-WW2 generation now have the wisdom of maturity, and the wherewithal of knowledge to speak out forthrightly in the political process to hold political villains of all parties accountable for the treachery of governance that has the audacity to lay claim to virtue yet lacks the strength to admit a mistake, lacks the humility to accept blame and remains wholly unaccountable for its vices, **UNTIL NOW.**

In the early to mid-70's, I met a man who was President of the Veterans of Foreign Wars. During our discussion, I asked him about his politics. I shall always remember his words of wisdom, "I always vote against the incumbent." Elective government is fallacious and immoral when it disregards the will of its constituents. Policies of sovereign democracies or republics are predicated on hypocrisy if they disregard the sovereignty of other governments. "Methods of thought which claim to give the lead to our world in the name of revolution have become, in reality, ideologies of consent and not of rebellion" – Albert Camus. Elected officials derive their power from the consent of the governed and they dishonor themselves and their office when they disregard or betray the consent of their constituents. Such betrayal should be constitutionally considered a "high crime", an impeachable offense. Seemingly over the last forty years, with matters still as they are **IT IS TIME TO THROW THE BASTARDS OUT.** Politicians are like diapers. They should be changed frequently and for the same reason. For those of us who still have flowers in our hearts, if not in our hair, we can still remake the world if we unite with purpose, the idealism of our youth and the wisdom of our years.

This trilogy of work advocates for consent toward the recognition and realization of the parallel goals of freedom of spirit from the bonds of religious dogma, political ideology, and freedom of body from bonds of economic restraint, i.e. complete sovereignty of soul and body. Homo Divinitas need not cede spiritual sovereignty to any institution or anyone. Homo Divinitas will however, have unlimited access to all knowledge, theologies, and philosophies, in order to self-ordain his or her search for the Great Integrity. Homo Divinitas should enjoy freedom from the restrictions of financial-value restraint that represents bondage, or in some cases, an addiction, to pleasures and/or self-gratification. On one hand, bonds of economics deprive the financially indigent from enjoying the basic necessities of life. On the other hand, economic bonds deprive wealthy persons of life's simplest and most sublime happiness because financial riches are ill used toward the pursuit of ever more pleasure and self-gratification. "Where wealth accumulates, men decay." – Oliver Goldsmith (1730 – 1774).

Quoting Maximilien Robespierre (1758 – 1794), one of the leading figures in the French Revolution, "What is the end of our revolution? The tranquil enjoyment of liberty and equality; the reign of that eternal justice, the laws of which are graven, not on marble or stone, but in the hearts of men, even in the heart of the slave who has forgotten them, and in that of the tyrant who disowns them." The basic premise of the trilogy is that spiritually, a prince is no different than a beggar. Truth is an equally daunting adversary for slave and king, beggar and prince. Verily the slave who abides Truth is a king; the ruler who does not abide Truth is a beggar. May the slave of spirit who has forgotten his divinity have the courage to reclaim such. May the tyrant gain strength and wisdom to deign power in favor of benevolence. May each of us who have unrequited dreams have the courage to reclaim them and make them real. Just as importantly, perhaps even more so may we, each of us of the Age of Aquarius, encourage those younger than us to dream. For, if we have not the opportunity to accomplish our own dreams, perhaps we can plow furrows in the fields enabling seeds of dreams of others to come to fruition.

I choose to close this work with the same words that closed *A New Reformation*. Hindus and people of the Himalayas verbalize the term 'Namaste' as a form of greeting/blessing. The origin of "namaste" (pronounced nahmastay) is ancient Sanskrit. Namaste essentially means, "the divinity in me recognizes the divinity in you." In using the blessing, one presses both hands together, palms touching, held near the heart, with head slightly bowed. The hands held in union signify oneness in the universe of duality, the bonding of spirit and matter.

Truth can be defined in yet another way for infinity has many facets. The Bengali poet Rabindranath Tagore was a poet of substantial note who won the Nobel Prize for Literature in 1913. Amidst the Mohandas K. Gandhi Memorial in New Delhi a stone bears the following inscription by Tagore as he honors Gandhiji. "He stopped at the thresholds of the huts of the thousands of dispossessed, dressed like one of their own. He spoke to them in their own language. Here was a living truth at last, and not from the quotations from books. For this reason, the mahatma, the name given to him by the people of India, is his real name. Who else has felt like him that all Indians are his own flesh and blood? When love came to the door of India, that door was opened wide. At Gandhi's call India blossomed forth to new greatness. Just as once before, in earlier times, when Buddha proclaimed the truth of fellow-feelings and compassion among all living creatures."

Chapter one began with a definition of Truth. This author will choose to finish this work by quoting Tielhard de Chardin when he spoke of the magnificence of Homo Divinitas. "But, as the facts prove only too well, this first way of believing in Man goes hand in hand with another way, more elementary, immediate and simple, and therefore more alluring. Correctly interpreted, I repeat, faith in Man can and indeed must cast us at the feet and arms of One who is greater than ourselves. But, it can be argued, why after all should we not conceive this One who is greater than ourselves as being in fact identical with ourselves? Given the power he possesses, why should Man look for a God outside himself? Man, self-sufficient and wholly autonomous, sole master and disposer of his destiny and the world's – is not this an even nobler concept?"[43]

Truths can be found whether in Walt Whitman, Janis Joplin, Sir Thomas More, or ancient Sanskrit blessings. The beauty is when, in that journey, you find the Holy Grail as the divinity within *yourself*. May you find Shangri-La, whatever you perceive it to be, and may you understand the blessings during your journey. Namaste.

Author's note: Thoughts and beliefs contained in my work express what I consider to be the expression of my spiritual sovereignty. I do not presume to tell anyone what to do or believe because each person has the divine right to determine their own path to answer their own calling. *Toward Spiritual Sovereignty* is also not intended to be a monologue. The author welcomes participants into this discussion of spirituality by posting comments and observations on the johncasperson.com website. With expanding and continuing dialog, each person maybe assist other toward the realization that force is the expression of weakness and wisdom and forbearance the full measure of strength. The light of knowledge and wisdom from masters past and present can help eradicate the cancers of ignorance, hate, and violence, and in their stead, endow a legacy of peace and understanding for future generations of Homo Divinitas.

Endnotes

[1] Durant, Will. The Life of Greece. New York, N.Y., Simon & Schuster, 1966, p.350.

[2] http://en.wikipedia.org/wiki/Truth. January 1, 2007.

[3] Martin, William. The Best Liberal Quotes Ever. Naperville, Il. Sourcebooks, 2004, p.248.

[4] Riley-Smith, Jonathan. The Crusades: A History; Second Edition. New Haven and London. Yale Nota Bene, 2005, p. xxxiii.

[5] Tolle, Eckhart. A New Earth. New York, Penguin Group, 2005, pp.74-75.

[6] Winfrey, Oprah. O The Oprah Magazine, January 2007 Volume 8 Number 1, New York, p. 160 & p. 217.

[7] Ducker, Donna and Evan. Buddy Booby's Birthmark. USA. 2006, p. Foreward.

[8] Ducker, Donna and Evan. Buddy Booby's Birthmark. USA. 2006, p. Notes

[9] Durant, Will and Ariel. The Age of Napoleon. New York, Simon & Schuster, 1975, p. 579.

[10] Durant, Will. The Story of Philosophy. USA, The Pocket Library, 1926, p. 202.

[11] Pagels, Elaine. The Origin of Satan. USA. Bookspan, 2005, p. 164.

[12] Gibran, Khalil. Sand and Foam. New York, Alfred A, Knopf, 1926, p. 77.

[13] Vicente, Mark, & Chasse, Betsy & Arntz, William. What the Bleep Do We Know. Captured Light & Lord of the Films, LLC. 2004.

[14] May, Dr. Rollo. Man's Search for Himself. New York, Dell Publishing. 1953, p.14.

[15] May, Dr. Rollo. Man's Search for Himself. New York, Dell Publishing. 1953, pp.14-15.

[16] Casperson, John. A New Reformation. New York, Vantage Press.

2006, p.15.

[17] Casperson, John. A New Reformation. New York, Vantage Press. 2006, pp.15-16.

[18] Tolle, Eckhart. A New Earth. New York, Penguin Group, 2005, p. 213.

[19] Durant, Will. The Life of Greece. New York, Simon & Schuster, 1966, p. 354.

[20] Ruiz, Miguel Angel. The Four Agreements: A Toltec Wisdom. (Audio Book). San Rafael, Ca.

[21] Morrow, Lance. Evil. Time Magazine Vol. 137 No. 23. New York, 1991, pp. 50-51.

[22] Brzezinski, Zbigniew. Out of Control. Collier Books, Macmillan Publishing, New York, 1993, p. 17.

[23] MacCullough, Diarmaid. The Reformation: A History. Penguin Group, 2003. p. 610.

[24] MacCullough, Diarmaid. The Reformation: A History. Penguin Group, 2003. pp. 610-611.

[25] Durant, Will. The Age of Faith. New York. Simon and Schuster, 1950. p. 185.

[26] Durant, Will. The Age of Faith. New York. Simon and Schuster, 1950. p. 360.

[27] Durant, Will. The Age of Faith. New York. Simon and Schuster, 1950. p. 186.

[28] Berry, Carmen Rene. The Unauthorized Guide to Sex and The Church. Nashville, Tennessee. W. Publishing Group, 2005, p. 83.

[29] Berry, Carmen Rene. The Unauthorized Guide to Sex and The Church. Nashville, Tennessee. W. Publishing Group, 2005, p. 82.

[30] Berry, Carmen Rene. The Unauthorized Guide to Sex and The Church. Nashville, Tennessee. W. Publishing Group, 2005, p. 80.

[31] www.bookrgas.com/notes/uto/PART14.htm.

[32] Gibran, Khalil. Sand and Foam. New York, Alfred A, Knopf, 1926, p. 71.

[33] Armstrong, Karen. A History of God. New York, Gramercy Books, 1993, p. 375.

[34] Armstrong, Karen. A History of God. New York, Gramercy Books, 1993, p. 376.

[35] Nietzsche, Friedrich. Thus Spake Zarathustra, A Book for Every

One and No One. Trans, R.J. Hollingdale, London, 1961, p. 217.

[36] Durant, Will. The Age of Faith. New York, Simon & Schuster, 1950. p. 53.

[37] Durant, Will. The Age of Faith. New York, Simon & Schuster, 1950. p. 52.

[38] Durant, Will. The Age of Faith. New York, Simon & Schuster, 1950. p. 517.

[39] Armstrong, Karen. A History of God. New York. Gramercy Books. 1993, p. 356.

[40] Armstrong, Karen. A History of God. New York. Gramercy Books. 1993, p. 357.

[41] www.newadvent.org/cathen/14520c.htm. (Catholic Encyclopedia)

[42] www.geocities.com/tertulliancyprian/31.htm. (Tertullian:31 On the Nature of the Soul)

[43] de Chardin, Pierre Tielhard. The Future of Man. USA. Image Book published by Doubleday. 2004, p. 182.

www.ingramcontent.com/pod-product-compliance
Lightning Source LLC
Chambersburg PA
CBHW061348280526
45784CB00001B/178